Charlestown Navy Yard

Boston National Historical Park
Massachusetts

Produced by the
Division of Publications
National Park Service

U.S. Department of the Interior
Washington, DC

CONSTITUTION

Following pages: *Boston Harbor, about 1870. Visible in the foreground are Charlestown Navy Yard's timber dock* (left) *and dry dock* (center left, with docked vessel). *The ships anchored off the navy yard piers are* (left) *U.S.S.* Ohio, *the yard's receiving ship (for housing recruits and sailors transferring between vessels), and U.S.S.* Wabash *"in ordinary" (that is, out of commission and in storage).*

Pages 6-7: *In 1803, U.S.S.* Constitution *was careened at a Boston wharf for recoppering before sailing for the Mediterranean to confront the Barbary States.*

Contents

*D*eep within Boston Harbor, Charlestown Navy Yard was birthplace, repair center, outfitting base, and port of refuge for thousands of U.S. naval vessels. This is the story of the yard, the ships it served, and the people who kept them seaworthy.

Part 1

The Making of a Navy

U.S. Naval Shipyards

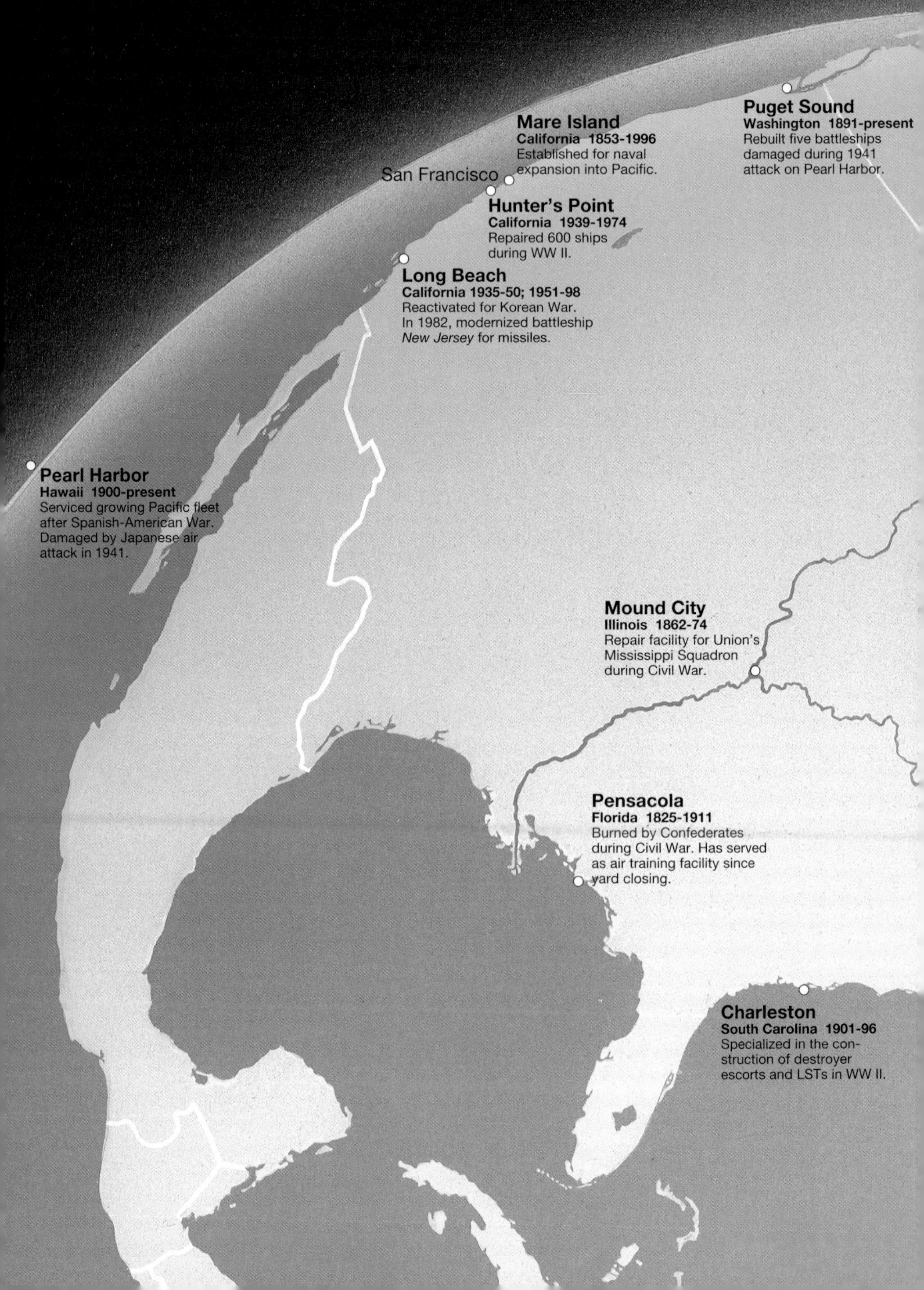

Mare Island
California 1853-1996
Established for naval
expansion into Pacific.

Puget Sound
Washington 1891-present
Rebuilt five battleships
damaged during 1941
attack on Pearl Harbor.

San Francisco

Hunter's Point
California 1939-1974
Repaired 600 ships
during WW II.

Long Beach
California 1935-50; 1951-98
Reactivated for Korean War.
In 1982, modernized battleship
New Jersey for missiles.

Pearl Harbor
Hawaii 1900-present
Serviced growing Pacific fleet
after Spanish-American War.
Damaged by Japanese air
attack in 1941.

Mound City
Illinois 1862-74
Repair facility for Union's
Mississippi Squadron
during Civil War.

Pensacola
Florida 1825-1911
Burned by Confederates
during Civil War. Has served
as air training facility since
yard closing.

Charleston
South Carolina 1901-96
Specialized in the con-
struction of destroyer
escorts and LSTs in WW II.

Prologue

The U.S. government established Charlestown Navy Yard as the newly-formed republic was meeting early challenges to its merchant shipping. In the decade after gaining independence, the young nation kept no standing navy. But continuing raids on U.S. commerce by Barbary pirates and French privateers in the 1790s spurred Congress to authorize the construction of new warships.

Realizing that existing private shipyards were inadequate for the increasingly ambitious shipbuilding program, the Secretary of the Navy established in 1800–1801 six federal yards to build, outfit, repair, and supply naval vessels. These facilities at Portsmouth, N.H.; Boston; New York; Philadelphia; Washington, D.C.; and Norfolk, Va., were the nucleus of the naval shipyard system. Except during the Civil War, they launched most of the Navy's vessels until the advent of steel hulls in the 1880s, when private yards began building them in greater numbers.

As with the first six, later naval shipyards were sometimes created to fill an immediate military need. The War of 1812, for instance, prompted the building of the two Great Lakes yards. The Mound City yard was established during the Civil War, strategically located near the confluence of the Mississippi and Ohio Rivers to build and repair Union gunboats. Although U.S. naval vessels are today built in private shipyards, four navy yards still actively serve the fleet.

Strategically located Great Lakes shipyards built gunboats and sloops during the War of 1812.

Erie ○
Presque Isle
Pennsylvania
1812-25

Sackets Harbor
New York 1812-1870s

Washington
District of Columbia
1800-83
○

New York
Brooklyn
New York
1800-1966

Portsmouth
New Hampshire
1800-present
○

Philadelphia
Pennsylvania
1801-1996
○

○ Boston
Charlestown
Massachusetts
1800-1974

○
Norfolk
Virginia 1801-present
Of the six original navy yards, only Norfolk and Portsmouth still service naval vessels.

New London
Connecticut 1868-83
During WW I was developed as major submarine base.

9

Growth of the Yard

When Captain William Bainbridge arrived in Boston aboard U.S.S. (United States Ship) *Constitution* in February 1813, he had reason to be satisfied. While the U.S. Army faltered early in the War of 1812, a string of naval victories over British ships was boosting public confidence. Two months earlier, the big frigate commanded by Bainbridge had engaged H.M.S. (His Majesty's Ship) *Java* off the coast of Brazil. *Java* was the faster ship, but *Constitution* had heavier guns. By skillful maneuvering, *Constitution* kept them trained on the British frigate, pounding *Java* with broadsides until its colors came down.

Crew and commander were met with parades in Boston, but Bainbridge had little time to enjoy the acclaim. He was immediately faced with a task that, if not as exciting as a sea battle, was nevertheless formidable. He had temporarily relinquished command of the Charlestown Navy Yard when he sailed on *Constitution*. While he was gone, Navy Secretary Paul Hamilton charged the yard with building one of the nation's first ships-of-the-line—the battleships of their day. As things now stood, that was an impossibility: Charlestown simply lacked the facilities for such an undertaking.

Bainbridge, who at 37 had already seen extensive naval action and been imprisoned by Barbary pirates, wrote soon after becoming commandant in 1812: "No period of my naval life has been more industrious or fatiguing." He was shorthanded and hampered by bad weather, conditions that must have sorely tested the endurance of a man with his temperament: aggressive,

Captain William Bainbridge was the Charlestown yard's second commandant (1812-15) and captain of the first ship built there, U.S.S. Independence.
Preceding pages: *1833 view of one of the yard's wharves, by William Bennett. Beyond, decommissioned* Independence *and* Columbus *are roofed over for protection.*

volatile, not noted for his patience. When he took command of the Charlestown yard, Bainbridge pressed the Washington bureaucracy to authorize improvements to a facility that suffered, in his words, from "mismanagement and neglect."

Years later, Bainbridge was typically blunt in depicting for the Secretary of the Navy what he saw as the Herculean task assigned him in 1812. The yard had been "in a state of perfect chaos. The public property in a state of ruin and decay...a boat could not approach at certain periods of the tide within five hundred feet of the shore...it was even exposed to the inroads of the cattle from [the] highway."

Even allowing for Bainbridge's penchant for the dramatic, his description was accurate. The buildings were too few, too small, and in need of repair. The timber needed to complete the repair of the frigate *Chesapeake* was decayed beyond use. But most pressing was the need for a large stone wharf and building slip. Here was a naval shipyard that could not service a sloop-of-war, let alone build a large frigate or ship-of-the-line. Small vessels could tie up at the modest wooden wharf, but the yard had to rent private wharves for repairing warships. *Chesapeake* had been languishing since 1809 in a rented berth at $1500 a year.

The commandant's hilltop house surveyed 25 acres of scattered buildings and grassy tidal flats directly across the "stream" (the Charles River) from Boston. There was a marine barracks, a parade ground, carpenter and blacksmith shops, a timber shed, a small hospital, a saltwater timber dock, and piles of cannon, shot, iron, and ballast. The facility Bainbridge took over in 1812 was in truth more supply depot than shipyard.

So why, after his exploits aboard *Constitution,* when another ship command and the chance for further glory were his for the asking, did Bainbridge return to

Charlestown? Because he had also asked to command the powerful 74-gun ship-of-the-line the yard would build, and he wanted to oversee construction.

On resuming command in March 1813 he lobbied again for a wharf and building slip. As a well-known ship's captain he was used to getting the attention of the Navy Department. But his sphere of activity had shifted from quarterdeck to desktop, and he had to watch coveted funds go to ships bound for sea. He was not, however, one to hold his tongue. He bombarded the Secretary of the Navy with letters (the tone of which, in this and other matters, sometimes bordered on sarcasm) until the wharf and slip were finally begun in April 1813. After the laying of the 74's keel in May, Bainbridge was relentless in his requests for more improvements—a navy store, capstans for hauling out ships, "shears" (a simple crane) for installing masts, a ropewalk.

But his real passion was the great ship he could watch taking shape from his window. He even suggested the name: *Independence.* Bainbridge chafed to "give John Bull an opportunity of testing the strength of an American 74"—especially after *Chesapeake* had finally left the yard in June only to be captured practically within sight of Boston by the British frigate *Shannon.*

The combative commandant was rarely put off by obstacles—or someone else's reputation. Having clashed with workers over compensation they demanded for days lost to bad weather, he shut out the source of trouble by ordering a shiphouse 210 feet long and 50 feet high built over the 74's building slip. To oversee ship construction Bainbridge hired Edmund Hartt and his son Edward—well-regarded Boston shipbuilders in whose yard was built the hugely successful *Constitution.* But in a dispute with Edward Hartt the angry Bainbridge grabbed him "by the

shoulder and carried him out of my office." Hartt's father quit in protest, whereupon Bainbridge quickly engaged another shipbuilder to finish the job.

Bainbridge's other main duty as commander of the yard was the defense of Boston Harbor—the importance of which was underscored by the *Shannon-Chesapeake* engagement. By spring of 1814 British warships were raiding the New England coast almost at will, and the Boston citizenry (many of whom vigorously opposed the war) was anxious over an anticipated attack on the city. The rising 74, Bainbridge knew, made a tempting target while it was unarmed and immobile on the ways. He asked for the New England Guards, a Boston militia company, to stand ready at the yard as *Independence* neared completion.

Guarding United States property at the Charlestown yard was normally the responsibility of the U.S. Marines, stationed there since 1802. But it was a small detachment, not enough to defend the yard and its ships against a serious attack. Bainbridge, who earlier protested the vulnerability of the yard, had other problems with the marines. Though they were under naval command while at sea, on shore the Navy had no authority over them. Bainbridge deplored this situation, complaining that his inability to mete out the same corporal punishment to marines as was used on sailors was "productive of insubordination."

In any case *Independence* was ready for launching by June 1814. But the much-anticipated ceremony on the 18th was an embarrassing failure. *Independence* hung up halfway down the launching ways, much to the satisfaction of a Federalist quoted in the *Boston Gazette:* "It was no wonder she stuck...the war itself sticks." The next day, when workers attempted to move the vessel by winch with the New England Guards pitching in to haul

U.S.S. Independence, *built at Charlestown in 1815, was the nation's first ship-of-the-line. On its maiden voyage the 74-gun vessel served as flagship of the Mediterranean squadron in the Barbary Wars.*

After the Charlestown yard removed one gun deck in 1835, turning the slow 74 into a fast, powerful frigate (above), Independence served as flagship of the Brazil and Pacific squad-

rons. The frigate spent the last 60 years of its career as receiving ship (temporary sailors' quarters) at Mare Island Navy Yard near San Francisco Bay, where it ended a century of service in 1914.

Ships-of-the-Line *were the battleships of their day, carrying 64 to 100 guns or more on two or three gun decks (below the open decks). Ship-rigged (square sails on three masts), these warships took their place in the line of battle in large fleet actions.*

Frigates *had 22 to 44 guns on one gun deck. They were ship-rigged counterparts of today's cruisers, excelling in single engagements and as commerce destroyers. Frigates also did convoy duty and served as scouts for battle fleets.*

Sloops-of-War *had 8 to 24 guns on an open deck and were ship-rigged. Fast and versatile—the destroyers of their day—sloops provided escort protection and harassed enemy shipping. Their shallow draft made them useful in coast defense and in lake squadrons.*

Brigs-of-War *had about 20 smaller guns on an open gun deck and carried square sails on two masts. Designed as small, fast cruisers, they served as scouts, blockade runners, commerce raiders, and in anti-piracy and slaveship patrols.*

on the lines, a block flew apart and killed master joiner William Champney.

Then, to worsen an already grim situation, the British warships that had blockaded Boston Harbor for over a year became an immediate threat. A raiding party from the frigate *Nymphe* rowed into the harbor in the early morning darkness of the 21st and burned a small sloop within a mile of the yard. The next day, with the charred remains of the vessel tied up at a Charlestown wharf, the leader of the raid publicly taunted Bainbridge. In an open letter in the *Boston Patriot*, Bainbridge was warned to better defend his "unfledged Independence."

On the afternoon of June 22, under the eye of the Guards, the vessel finally slid down the ways into Boston Harbor. The launching was celebrated by a gun salute from *Constitution* and cheers from a crowd of 20,000. Bainbridge's friend, the author Washington Irving, couldn't attend but wrote Bainbridge that he would drink a "potation bottle...to the success of your first cruise." In the same spirit Bainbridge entertained with food and drink 300 mechanics and laborers who had, he said, "worked cheap, and done their work most faithfully."

But the war he wanted so badly to join remained out of Bainbridge's reach. Desertions, along with financial and outfitting delays, held up the vessel until 1815, by which time peace with England had been concluded.

Another opportunity soon presented itself. The predatory corsairs of the North African Barbary States—Tunisia, Tripolitania, Algeria, and Morocco—had long been a thorn in the side of American merchant shipping. Bainbridge, with *Independence* as his flagship, won command of a squadron whose mission was to display to the Barbaries the new power of the U.S. Navy. The assignment was particularly attractive to Bainbridge, who

earlier in his career had surrendered a ship to the Tripolitans and had another commandeered by the Algerians. But a second squadron under Captain Stephen Decatur beat Bainbridge across the Atlantic and defeated the Algerians in battle. His role was thus reduced to persuading the other Barbaries at gunpoint to end their extortionist ways. The suppression of the Barbary pirates was nevertheless satisfying to Bainbridge. As senior officer, he had the honor of commanding the squadron that initiated a permanent U.S. presence in the Mediterranean—the first of the Navy's "distant station" squadrons.

Upon Bainbridge's return to Boston he attempted to regain command of the yard from his replacement, Captain Isaac Hull. Unsuccessful, he was instead appointed Port Captain ("commander afloat" of all naval vessels in Boston Harbor), with *Independence* designated station flagship. Bainbridge settled down to a career as a senior officer, serving as commandant at the yard twice more in the 1820s and '30s. He had helped put Charlestown on the map as the builder of a major warship. More significantly, after the War of 1812 the yard began building a reputation as an important repair and supply facility.

The Charlestown yard, and the U.S. Navy itself, owed their existence in part to the same Barbary pirates who occasioned *Independence's* first cruise. The severing of ties with Britain during the Revolution also meant the loss of protection from the Barbaries long provided by the Mother Country's powerful navy and by the "tribute" Britain paid them. The United States had no navy to protect its seaborne commerce—so essential to a coastal nation dependent on overseas trade—and the treasury could not bear the tribute payments or the ransom demands for captured ships and sailors.

Thus after independence the Mediterranean trade had been virtually closed to the United States. There was much unresolved debate about the problem, but when the pirates spilled out into the Atlantic in 1793 and took 11 American vessels in a few months, Congress took action. The following year it authorized six frigates, three of which were launched in 1797: *United States, Constellation,* and *Constitution.*

Congress was spurred to finish the job by the actions of Revolutionary France during its war with Britain. French commerce raiders so terrorized American neutral shipping that in 1798 an angry U.S. government created the Navy Department and prepared for war. (There were a number of engagements at sea, but war was never declared.) Congress authorized funds to build, borrow, or accept as gifts 49 vessels, ranging from galleys to six 74-gun ships-of-the-line.

The 74s were never built, but while the program was still alive, naval shipyards to build them were established in Portsmouth, Boston, New York, Philadelphia, Washington, and Norfolk. Boston, wrote Secretary of the Navy Benjamin Stoddert to President John Adams, from "the natural strength of its situation [meaning its large, deep, and defensible harbor], the great number of ship carpenters in its vicinity, and of its seamen, must always remain a building place and place of rendezvous for our navy of the first importance." Thus in 1800 the Charlestown Navy Yard was established.

For most of its history Charlestown's primary mission was to keep the fleet sailing. That is not to say the yard wasn't a shipbuilder; it built more than 200 warships over its 174 years of operation. But most of the new ships were built to meet the immediate demands of war. (Three quarters of them were launched during World War II alone.) For fully half of those years no new ships came down the ways. The pattern established in the yard's early years was one of ongoing repair, outfitting, supply, and conversion work punctuated by occasional new launchings.

The classes of ships that came down the ways at Charlestown and other naval yards were the outcome of strategic and political deliberations in Washington. U.S. naval policy devised during the first half of the 19th century had its roots in the War of 1812. Before the British blockade bottled up its warships, the tiny U.S. Navy had successfully fought a brief *guerre de course* against Britain, using a strategy that emphasized single ship actions and raids on enemy shipping with relatively small, fast frigates and sloops-of-war. The early naval successes prompted Congress in 1813 to authorize six new frigates (three of which were built) and six sloops. These, and the nine frigates authorized in 1816 and laid down in the 1820s (including the Charlestown-built *Cumberland*), formed the backbone of the Navy until just before the Civil War.

But the War of 1812, which helped shape a practical role for the 19th-century Navy, also led lawmakers into an expensive attempt to compete with European navies on their terms. Using the argument that large, powerful ships were essential to the defense of the nation's shores (and perhaps remembering the crucial role of French 74s at Yorktown), Congress also authorized four 74-gun ships-of-the-line in the 1813 act.

While ships-of-the-line were traditionally used in fleet actions with set lines of battle (hence their name), they were also deployed to break blockades and to "show the flag"—that is, remind other nations of the United States' military reach. Postwar nationalism, a popular navy still basking in the nation's praise, and the country's demonstrated vulnerability to blockade prompted appropriations in 1816 for additional 74s.

Between 1813 and 1822 fourteen 74s were laid down, including *Independence* (1813), *Vermont* (1818), and *Virginia* (1822) at Charlestown. But in the decade after the war strategists cast a skeptical eye on such large ships. The expensive, provocative, and easily outmaneuvered behemoths, they said, were only a drag on the Navy—inappropriate for a young nation that wanted to stay out of European conflicts. By 1825 only five 74s had gone into service.

In 1835 *Independence* took a turn in its career that was emblematic of naval policy. The 74 had lain idle at Charlestown for 13 years. It was a sluggish sailer, and its great weight and design flaws brought the lower lee guns too close to the water to be useful during combat. So *Independence* was "razeed," cut down from three decks to two, and transformed from an unsuccessful ship-of-the-line into a very good 54-gun frigate—the largest and one of the fastest in the Navy.

Only a few present at its 1837 recommissioning realized that *Independence* was also among the last of its kind. Fast approaching was a technology that would displace naval sail; steam would drive the Navy of the future. In 1839 the Navy's first commissioned steamer—the two-year-old harbor battery *Fulton II*—arrived at Charlestown for repairs. A local paper called it "the oddest looking fish we have ever set our eyes on." Four towering stacks spouting black smoke rose from the deck, on which were mounted engine cylinders four feet in diameter. The sidewheel covers, likened to "immense fungi," barely cleared the sides of the dry dock.

With the dock and other improvements, the Charlestown yard had by the 1840s taken shape as an important repair and shipbuilding facility. The dry dock *(see pages 40-41)*, five years abuilding, had opened in 1833 amid much ceremony. Vice President Martin Van Buren and other dignitaries watched as the already-venerable *Constitution,* stripped and demasted, inaugurated the dock. Much of the tidal flats had been reclaimed behind a granite quay (the yard would triple its original size by 1869), and the rest of the yard's uneven grounds had been leveled. A high stone wall, built to help stop pilfering and protect the ships, stretched between the Charles and Mystic rivers.

The yard had become more self-sufficient. The boilers for the dry dock pump engines also provided steam for the new sawmill and blockmaking and armorer's shops. In 1837, the yard's ropewalk (also steam-powered) and tar house had been completed *(see pages 20-21)*. The yard now made its own paint in the "oil house," while hardware was supplied by a large smithy with 12 forges.

Other significant additions: masting shears looming over the new shear wharf; a sparmaker's shed, masthouse, and sail loft; new timber docks; a steam chest for bending wood; an armory with thousands of muskets, bayonets, and swords; and neat ranks of guns, shot, and anchors in their respective "parks." Hundreds of elm trees planted by order of Commodore Bainbridge softened the yard's industrial setting.

Anchored out in the harbor were several vessels "in ordinary." A vessel in ordinary was out of service and in storage with a skeleton crew until recommissioned. The ship was demasted, salted to retard dry rot, whitewashed inside, tightly caulked, and its sides and decks "payed" with a thick coat of varnish and tar. Tubular windsails directing air belowdecks and holes cut in the bulkheads insured good air circulation. Some vessels in ordinary at Charlestown had protective wood and canvas sheds over their decks, an innovation of Captain Hull.

Vermont, Virginia, and the frigate *Cumberland,* begun in 1825, had become permanent fixtures in their great shiphouses. They were still officially under construction and near completion, but were really in ordinary. (*Virginia* was something of an ill-starred vessel. Over the years at least three people had died in accidents around the ship, and its reputation was reconfirmed in 1845 when a visitor fell to his death from its scaffolding.) Construction on *Virginia* and *Vermont* had slowed to a standstill after critics questioned the strategic value of ships-of-the-line. But economic considerations played at least as big a role; ordinary was a cheap way to keep expensive-to-sail vessels, including big frigates like *Cumberland* (launched in 1842), ready for war.

In 1848 *Vermont* was finally launched to "a vast concourse of people and the firing of cannons." But the day of the big 74s was over. Neither *Vermont* nor *New Hampshire* (built at Portsmouth Navy Yard), the last two ships-of-the-line completed by the Navy, ever saw service as a commissioned warship. In fact most 74s had short careers of little strategic consequence. *Independence,* first of the class, was the only one still serving as a warship at mid-century, but it had been cut down to a frigate.

The launching of *Vermont* also closed a chapter in the yard's history. The second ship laid down at Charlestown 30 years before, *Vermont* was the last all sail-powered warship launched there—obsolescent even as it came down the ways.

Although this was a U.S. Navy Yard run by naval officers, throughout its history those wielding the caulking mallets and rivet guns were civilians working for civilian foremen. During the first half of the 19th century the yard's workforce steadily increased from 89 in 1822 to 370 in 1853. At mid-century the records show most of them were born in New England—half from Massachusetts. Some 15 percent were Irish, the majority working as laborers.

So complicated an undertaking as the building of a warship required an array of specialized occupations falling under the general label of "mechanics": carpenters, sawyers, joiners, sparmakers, blockmakers, painters, gun carriage makers, armorers, sailmakers, blacksmiths, caulkers, riggers, boatbuilders, coopers, ropemakers, masons, machinists, plumbers, and coppersmiths. A force of unskilled laborers was at times supplemented by the ordinary crews and by the sailors stationed at the yard.

Each shop had its master, quartermen (leaders of several crews), leadingmen (crew leaders), and crews of mechanics, apprentices, laborers, and a few boys (before child labor laws eliminated such positions). In the early years, when the yard's facilities were sparse, it was not unusual for the master to have his own shop outside of the yard. The commandant would in effect contract with the master to do the work there with his own men. In the 1840s and '50s the Navy tightened the regulations, giving the masters less leeway in hiring and ordering supplies. By the Civil War they were all yard employees.

A look at the young men in the apprenticeship program, started in 1817, gives a clearer picture of the yard employees they would become. Those applying for the program—generally at age 16—had to show good character and be physically able to perform the tasks of their trade. They had to demonstrate the ability to read, write, and do simple math. The terms of the five-year indenture (later reduced to four) were generally clear: in return for exhibiting growing mastery of his trade, the apprentice received from the Navy room and board, increasing pay, and continuing education in reading, writing, arithmetic, and

Navy Yard Tradesmen in the Age of Sail

During the early 19th century, Charlestown's shipyard bell called several hundred civilian tradesmen and laborers to work each morning. Laboring from sunrise to sunset under the supervision of naval officers and civilian shop masters, these yard employees built, repaired, and supplied United States warships for naval duty around the globe. Fluctuating government budgets, changing seasons, and the uneven demands of war and peace made navy yard work intermittent and unpredictable. Below: A navy yard rigger tightens a warship's mast shrouds.

The Ropewalk

Several factors enticed the U.S. Navy into constructing its only ropemaking facility at the Charlestown Navy Yard in the 1830s: skilled labor, access to raw materials, and technical expertise. The port of Boston already boasted more than a dozen ropewalks employing many skilled artisans. Perhaps most importantly, the Navy was eager to take advantage of newly developed labor-saving machines like those already in use in New England's textile mills.

Because rope had to be twisted in a straight line, the maximum length that could be produced was determined by the length of the ropewalk (so called because workers spinning the hemp fibers by hand walked the length of the building). The Charlestown ropewalk's quarter-mile length allowed production of rope up to 1200 feet long. Designed by architect Alexander Parris (best known for Boston's Quincy Market), the ropewalk complex included

the rope "laying" area running the length of the building, spinning and preparing machine rooms, the hemp house, and the tar house. The complex was powered by massive steam engines and tended by men and boys. The Navy's move to mechanized rope production came at a critical time, as machine-spun rope began to replace intricate hand-spinning techniques. The hand spinners' resistance inspired contests in the 1840s, in which they

challenged the quality of machine-made rope. The results of such a challenge to the Charlestown ropewalk were somewhat ironic. Though its machine-made rope proved to be stronger and cheaper to produce, hand-spun rope was superior in the smaller sizes, and the mechanized ropewalk began producing some hand-spun rope, doing so until the end of the 19th century.

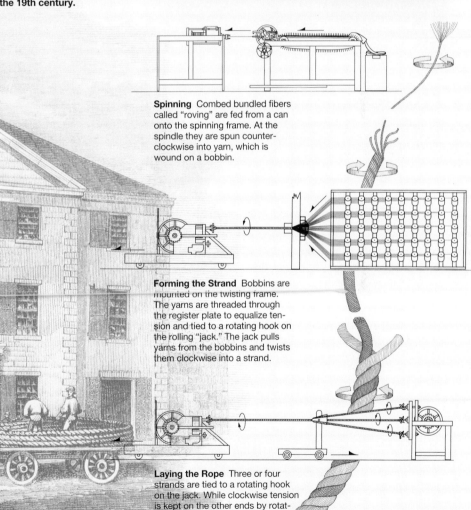

Spinning Combed bundled fibers called "roving" are fed from a can onto the spinning frame. At the spindle they are spun counter-clockwise into yarn, which is wound on a bobbin.

Forming the Strand Bobbins are mounted on the twisting frame. The yarns are threaded through the register plate to equalize tension and tied to a rotating hook on the rolling "jack." The jack pulls yarns from the bobbins and twists them clockwise into a strand.

Laying the Rope Three or four strands are tied to a rotating hook on the jack. While clockwise tension is kept on the other ends by rotating hooks, the strands are twisted counterclockwise into rope.

theories of the trade. But because the indenture was technically a personal contract between the boy's parents or guardian and the master, not the Navy, questions of obligation sometimes arose when a new man became master. At the end of the apprenticeship—usually at age 21—the boy became a yard employee.

Budget-minded Naval Commissioners in Washington allowed the commandant to pay just enough to hold on to his workers. He generally matched the rates of private shipyards in the area to keep workers from being lured away. The daily rates thus fell with the coming of cold weather and the slowing of work, since the workers were then in low demand elsewhere. The Navy defended this hardnosed practice, maintaining that with fewer daylight hours (workers mustered at sunrise and were dismissed at sunset), the yard got less work out of the men. The niggardly pay policies sometimes backfired: in 1821 the low-paid sailmakers left en masse to work at private yards.

More than the skilled craftsmen, the laborers' jobs depended on the amount of work at the yard, but most of the workforce awaited the coming of cold weather with some anxiety. The yard's practice was to retain only as many people as it could keep working, and bad weather sharply reduced the volume of work. The completion of a new ship or of a major repair job also meant the letting go of large numbers of workers, at least until the next job. In effect many in the workforce were not given permanent jobs, but only hired on to perform seasonal work, much like house carpenters, or to complete a single project.

Though the situation was normally weighted in favor of the employer, the scales could occasionally tip the other way, especially for skilled workers. In 1825, when the coming of spring coincided with a surge in building brought on by a recent Boston fire, Commandant William Crane was forced to raise wages to compete for skilled workers. He sent his Master Builder Josiah Barker up the coast as far as Portland to recruit mechanics.

At times skilled workers attempted to force the Navy's hand, organizing to protest conditions. When the caulkers struck for higher wages in January 1835, the commandant, Commodore Jesse Elliott, fired them and quickly found others willing to work at the established rate. Two days later the "refractory caulkers," unable to find work in the middle of the winter, asked to be rehired at their old wages. Wanting to remain on good terms with his employees, Elliott allowed the men to return.

Sometimes the walkout worked. Yard workers considered unreasonable a change in their working hours made in 1852. By this time they were working a straight 10-hour day. But under the new policy, they had to work sunrise to sunset if that period contained even a minute less than 11 hours, thus adding up to an hour to their day during the winter. They walked off the job, forcing the Navy to rescind the policy.

These actions represent a period when the yard workers, though not yet unionized, could strike—an option later denied to government employees. While workers were generally forced to accept the prevailing pay and conditions at the yard, they were not completely without power.

In the Charlestown Navy Yard's first half-century, world events, U.S. politics, and sectional rivalries affected the ebb and flow of work and the hiring and firing of men. The yard was born in the midst of a world at war and grew to prominence in a time of relative calm—in retrospect, the lull before the storm of civil war.

Sloop-of-war (U.S.S. Decatur *or* Dale*) dry docked in Charlestown has its rigging tarred and its hull sheathed with copper, about 1852.*

Building a Wooden Ship

The creation of a wooden warship began in the mold loft. There carpenters translated specifications from standard plans for each class of vessel into full-sized wooden patterns. These were used to fashion hull members, for which white oak or live oak were the favored woods. (Some 2,000 trees were required for a 74-gun ship-of-the-line.) On the slightly inclined building ways, joiners first laid the keel, the great spine of the ship running along the bottom of the hull. Then they attached the stem and the stern post to the keel and raised the frames—the vessel's ribs. The frames formed the contours of the hull and, together with horizontal deck beams and vertical stanchions beneath the beams, provided a strong skeleton. After 1829, iron and copper bolts and spikes replaced many of the wooden "treenails" that secured the structural members and fastened the deck and hull planking. The rudder was hung, the

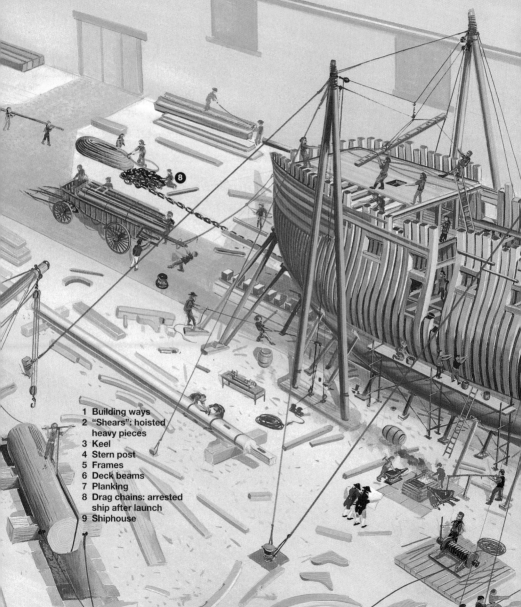

1 Building ways
2 "Shears": hoisted heavy pieces
3 Keel
4 Stern post
5 Frames
6 Deck beams
7 Planking
8 Drag chains: arrested ship after launch
9 Shiphouse

hull caulked and sheathed with copper to protect it from teredo worms, and the ship was launched. Riggers then "stepped" masts to the keelson, a lengthwise beam bolted to the keel *(see page 19)*. After they rigged the horizontal spars, cordage, and sails, the new warship was ready for outfitting.

The Workforce in 1835

138	Carpenters	16	Boatbuilders
56	Ropemakers	14	Sparmakers
40	Laborers	12	Blockmakers
37	Joiners	11	Painters
34	Blacksmiths	6	Caulkers
25	Sailmakers	6	Masons
19	Riggers	6	Sawyers
18	Coopers		
17	Plumbers		

Expanding U.S. interests in the Pacific spurred Congress in 1825 to authorize a new class of sloop-of-war to protect those interests. Charlestown Navy Yard constructed three of them between 1825 and 1827.

The Frigate *Constitution*

The first three warships ordered for the infant U.S. Navy in 1794—one of them the Boston-built *Constitution*—were frigates unlike any others. Naval strategists knew the nation could afford to build only a few vessels, so they had to be formidable warships. They were inspired by French "razees," ships-of-the-line *(see page 14)* that had one gun deck removed, transforming them into large, heavily armed frigates. The sharp

lines of *Constitution's* hull gave it a frigate's speed, but in size and stoutness it was comparable to a small ship-of-the-line. (Its heavy oak frames, spaced close together and sheathed with thick planking, proved virtually impenetrable in battle—hence the name "Old Ironsides.") The theory was that *Constitution* would be powerful enough to fight any frigate, quick enough to flee anything bigger. The British, though,

scorned the new frigates, asserting that they lacked the tactical strengths of either frigates or ships-of-the-line: too slow to engage the former, too weak to stand up to the latter. But *Constitution* more than lived up to U.S. expectations in the War of 1812, when it bested two British frigates in separate battles, escaped two more, and captured a frigate and a sloop-of-war in a third engagement. *Constitution*

The 24-Pounder Long Gun

A gun crew of 6 to 14 men wrestled with this 5,600-pound gun. To adjust elevation, a crew member placed a handspike on one of the steps (A) and levered the breech (B) up or down; the gun captain slid the quoin (C) in or out.

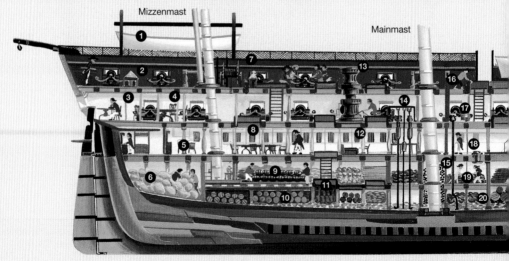

Mizzenmast

Mainmast

Specifications:
Length overall: 204 ft.
Beam (width): 43.5 ft.
Displacement: 2,200 tons
Draft: 22.5 ft.
Hull: 15 to 20 in. thick
Speed: 13-14 knots

Crew: 450-470
Armament in 1812: 30,
24-pounders; 22, 32-
pounder carronades;
two 24-pounder & one
18-pounder bow chasers
on the forecastle

1 Quarter boat
2 Quarterdeck
3 Captain's quarters
4 Captain's day cabin
5 Officers' staterooms
6 Bread room

7 Ship's wheel
8 Wardroom
9 Cartridge filling room
10 Powder magazine
11 Spirit room

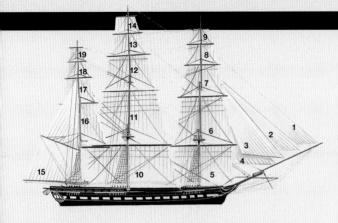

fought no more battles, but served honorably for another 40 years. Throughout its career *Constitution* has been closely associated with the Charlestown Navy Yard, undergoing several overhauls there. The first was in 1833, when the frigate inaugurated the yard's dry dock. In 1992-95 it was serviced in the same dock. Since 1897 the yard has been home port for *Constitution*, the Navy's oldest commissioned warship.

Constitution's Sails

Sail area, with studding sails (not shown), was more than 43,000 sq. ft.

1 Flying jib
2 Outer jib
3 Inner jib
4 Fore topmast staysail

5 Foresail
6 Fore topsail
7 Fore topgallant sail
8 Fore royal
9 Fore skysail
10 Mainsail
11 Main topsail
12 Main topgallant sail

13 Main royal
14 Main skysail
15 Spanker
16 Mizzen topsail
17 Mizzen topgallant sail
18 Mizzen royal
19 Mizzen skysail

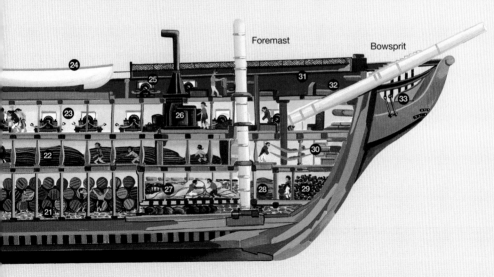

Foremast

Bowsprit

12 Cockpit (junior officers' quarters)
13 Anchor capstan
14 Bilge pumps
15 Shot locker
16 Spar deck (open)
17 Gun deck

18 Berthing deck (crew hung its hammocks on this deck)
19 Orlop deck (storage)
20 Hold
21 Ballast

22 Anchor cables
23 24-pounder guns
24 Long boat
25 32-pounder carronades
26 Galley
27 Sail locker

28 Sand room
29 Rigging blocks
30 Sick bay
31 Forecastle
32 Manger
33 Crew's head

The Coming of Iron and Steam

Merrimack, Virginia, Cumberland: names that point up the ironies of war. As the steam frigate *Merrimack* was being launched in July 1855 *(see pages 32-33),* the partially built ship-of-the-line *Virginia* lay in another part of the yard. It had been laid down and named in the 1820s, a more harmonious time. Even if the old 74 had finally come down the ways, it is not likely that, amidst the sectional acrimony of the 1850s, it would have kept the old name— and certainly not after the secession of the state whose namesake it was.

A year after *Merrimack's* launching, the frigate was back in the yard after going aground during its shakedown cruise (when the crew becomes familiar with a ship and problems are ironed out). While workers replaced damaged coppering and repaired the propeller on the big warship, a smaller sail frigate waited its turn.

Launched 13 years earlier, *Cumberland* had served as flagship of the African Squadron, whose mission was to suppress slave running. Now back home, *Cumberland* moved into the dry dock soon after *Merrimack* was towed out. It was cut down to a fast sloop-of-war with one gun deck of 28 guns and a crew of 376.

Cumberland's worth as a leaner warship was proven in the first months of the Civil War. Assigned to the Atlantic Blockading Squadron, the vessel took eight Confederate prizes in three weeks. But the next year *Cumberland,* among the last sailing ships launched by the Navy, came up hard against the future.

On March 8, 1862, *Cumberland* and other vessels were on blockade duty in Hamp-

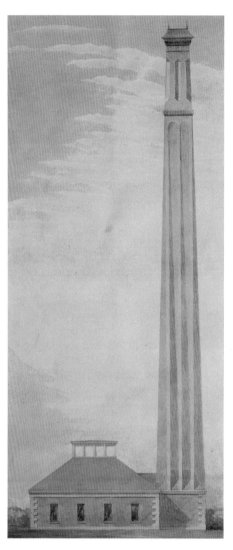

Architect's rendering of the Charlestown machine shop's "Great Chimney," 1858.
Preceding pages: *Sinking of Union sloop* Cumberland *by Confederate ironclad* Virginia *(ex-U.S.S.* Merrimack*) in 1862, by Alexander C. Stuart.*
Following pages: Merrimack *is launched at Charlestown in 1855;* Cumberland *was built in the same shiphouse in 1842.*

ton Roads, Virginia, when the men on deck sighted a bizarre new war machine steaming out of Norfolk. Approaching them was a dark, monolithic vessel—decks awash, no masts, no sails, no sailors. C.S.S. (Confederate States Ship) *Virginia,* the much-rumored ironclad blockade-breaker, had finally taken the stage.

It was a slow, clumsy vessel, but menacing nevertheless. Using a full mile to gather momentum, *Virginia* steamed steadily towards the Union vessels. It passed the frigate *Congress* and headed straight for *Cumberland,* its sloping iron casement shedding the Union ships' barrage of heavy shot and explosive shell as if they were "peas from a pop-gun," in the words of a *Cumberland* sailor. But *Cumberland,* though clearly outmatched, could not avoid engagement. It was at anchor in a dead calm, the crew's wash drying in the rigging. The Union sailors could only take the punishing return fire, clear the decks for battle, and wait for the inevitable.

Longer than *Cumberland* by half, with a submerged iron ram projecting from its bow, the approaching vessel looked to the Union ship's pilot like a "huge, half-submerged crocodile." *Virginia* tore into *Cumberland's* bow below the waterline *(see pages 28-29),* then backed off, leaving its ram imbedded in a seven-foot hole. Both vessels now loosed volleys at point-blank range; dozens of *Cumberland's* crew were maimed or killed.

As the vessel listed and began to sink, the crew abandoned ship, but 121 men—already dead, too hurt to save themselves, or firing guns to the end—went down with *Cumberland.* (As water flooded the gun deck, a young gun crew officer barely saved himself by squeezing through a gunport. He was Lieutenant Thomas Selfridge, who in 1890 became commandant of the Charlestown Navy Yard.) Before darkness ended the fighting, the ironclad also riddled *Congress,* killing more than a hundred men and setting the vessel on fire. *Congress* burned on into the night and finally exploded.

The frightening weapon that had handed the U.S. Navy its worst defeat began its career as the hull of a wooden steam vessel. A week after the surrender of Fort Sumter, the loss of the important Gosport Navy Yard at Norfolk to rebel troops became inevitable. Evacuating Union forces—under cover of *Cumberland*—burned and scuttled several warships to keep them from falling into Confederate hands. But some were salvageable, including a large steam frigate on which everything below the waterline was intact. Southern engineers converted the vessel into an advanced warship, removing the masts and topping the hull with a rooflike iron shell. The original name of the vessel they retrieved and transformed: U.S.S. *Merrimack.*

Merrimack's reincarnation as *Virginia* embodied two technologies—steam and iron (and then steel)—that were advanced during the Civil War and that eventually defined the modern Navy. Steam engineering had traveled a long road of acceptance in the conservative Navy. By 1850, the year the Charlestown Navy Yard built its first steamer, Great Britain had built or converted from sail some 25 propeller and paddlewheel steam warships. The U.S. Navy had launched only seven. Steam engines were still considered novelties by many old Navy men—at best auxiliary power, at worst dirty and undependable nuisances that called for machine tenders rather than sailors.

Their resistance was not entirely unjustified. There was the problem of range: *Merrimack,* for instance, could cruise only about 17 days with its coal bunker full. American steamers far from home had to depend on French or British coaling stations and machine shops in places like

Hong Kong and Shanghai. Unlike self-reliant sail, steam alone could not meet the demands of distant squadrons. And in the early days of steam, it was no faster than sail; in fact it was often slower. More crucial, early steam engines were inefficient and unreliable, so captains would not trust them in combat. And coal took up valuable space needed for supplies, crew, and ammunition.

But the main problem was that early steamers were driven by big, ungainly sidewheels that caused captains no end of problems *(see page 35).* They so harmed a vessel's sailing qualities that steam was of necessity the primary power source on sidewheelers—but the Navy wanted to use steam only as auxiliary power.

Another way of employing steam power for propulsion was needed. The propeller (called a "screw") was the answer, allowing naval steam to come into its own. Construction of the prototype screw sloop *Princeton* began in 1841, before America's first sidewheel warships even went into service. The Navy built only eight more deepwater sidewheelers before the famous 1854 class of six screw steamers (led by the Charlestown-built *Merrimack)* made the cumbersome vessels a footnote in naval history. With the advent of the propeller, enough problems were solved that auxiliary steam power became feasible in warships. On an 1858 cruise from Honolulu to Acapulco, *Merrimack* steamed only three days out of 32.

Merrimack, whose subsequent adventures we have already followed, was in the tradition of large American frigates like *Constitution.* While its engines were never very dependable, *Merrimack* was an excellent sailer, powerfully armed, and on its inaugural European cruise inspired Britain to build similar vessels with better engines.

The screw sloop *Hartford,* launched at Charlestown in 1858, was one of a follow-

up class of steamers. (These and other screw steamers of the '50s were all frigates and sloops; no steam ship-of-the-line was built at Charlestown or any other yard. As we have seen, the era of such large wooden ships was over by the time the Navy was converting to steam.) These were smaller vessels with a shallower draft—better suited to coastal and river operations. As Rear Admiral David G. Farragut's flagship in victories at New Orleans and Mobile Bay, *Hartford* was perhaps the most celebrated steamer in the Union Navy.

With propellers, even the most hidebound captains could appreciate the better maneuverability steam gave them during combat. Gradually the tactical roles of steam and sail were reversed, with increasingly efficient and dependable steam engines officially becoming the primary power source and sail the auxiliary. As a matter of economy, however, American vessels continued to use sail whenever possible on long-distance cruises.

Steam technology demanded a whole new set of skills of Charlestown's mechanics. When the steam battery *Fulton II* docked there in 1839, the yard could repair only the vessel's wooden components, having to contract work on the engine to local companies. But by 1845 yard personnel could fully service the screw sloop *Princeton.* While some carpenters may have made the transition, it is more likely that most of those working with steam machinery had a background in the field.

As the yard adapted to the new age, it underwent a decade of modernization and quickened production preceding the Civil War. The dry dock was lengthened; gas lights were installed; the yard began manufacturing wire rope in 1857. But the most important improvement was a state-of-the-art machine shop—its 240-foot stack long a landmark at the yard—that replaced the old smithery in 1859. It contained such equipment as a machine that could plane a metal surface 10 feet square and a huge lathe capable of handling iron propeller shafts 35 feet long. The facility also helped the yard to incorporate a new technology dramatized (though not introduced) by C.S.S. *Virginia:* ironcladding.

Sinking of large warships had rarely occurred in naval battle. Solid shot either bounced off thick wooden hulls or left a small, patchable hole. So warships normally just blasted away at each other until one of them, casualties mounting and its deck and rigging a shambles, hauled down its colors. Yet *Virginia* had sunk or caused to eventually sink two of them in two hours. Its ironcladding allowed it to get close enough to *Cumberland* to use an ancient but still effective technique, ramming, and close enough to *Congress* to pound the ship at close range with its broadside shot and big rifles. While ramming would not remain a tactical option, ironcladding was universally adopted as every naval power raced to design hulls that could withstand ever more powerful explosive shells fired from rifled guns *(see pages 42-43)*.

As in every war, technology helped shape strategy in the Civil War and strategic considerations helped determine how new technologies were applied. The Navy's major role in the war effort was to blockade some 3,500 miles of Southern coastline. The South's blockade runners were typically the most advanced examples of British shipbuilding, steam-powered sidewheelers that were often iron- or steel-hulled. In the first year of the war, only about one in eleven of these runners were caught (partly because sidewheelers were still faster than screw steamers), and the Union Navy continued to build, borrow, and buy every vessel it could to strengthen the blockade.

Thus when naval officers learned of the conversion of *Merrimack* into an armored blockade-breaker, they were understandably worried. In the debate over the type

Steam Propulsion

When steam was introduced as an auxiliary naval power source in the 1820s, paddlewheels were the initial method of propulsion. In the late 1830s engineers began working with propellers—"screws" in naval terminology. Each technology had its partisans: the sidewheel provided greater combat maneuverability, was suited to riverine warfare, and presented no problems of leakage, as did the screw's underwater shaft hole. However, the exposed wheels were vulnerable during combat, ate up deck space needed for guns, hindered sail handling, and created more drag than a screw when the vessel was under sail. The launching of the screw warships H.M.S. *Rattler* in Britain and U.S.S. *Princeton* in the United States in 1843 signaled the coming ascendancy of screw propulsion. In the historic 1845 tug-of-war between *Rattler* and an otherwise-identical sidewheeler, the greater efficiency of the screw was publicly confirmed.

1857 inboard plan of screw frigate Merrimack. *Screw could be hoisted into a well to reduce drag when the vessel was under sail.*

Sidewheels: good maneuverability, but vulnerable above the water.

The screw: more efficient, and protected below the waterline.

35

of vessel the Navy should develop to counter the Southern threat, John Ericsson's proposal for a turreted, shallow-drafted coastal ironclad won out over larger, oceangoing designs with traditional broadsides. His ironclad, called U.S.S. *Monitor*, was the prototype of the turreted ironclad class named after it. (While monitors and *Virginia*-type ironclads continued to meet the needs of a mostly coastal and riverine naval war, two broadside ironclads were built by the Union. One of them, *New Ironsides*, was quite effective.)

Monitor fought *Virginia* to a standoff the day after the latter sank *Cumberland*. It was the first clash between steam-powered ironclads, and the world took notice. Captain John Dahlgren, creator of *Monitor's* two big guns, put it succinctly: "Now comes the reign of iron—and cased sloops are to take the place of wooden ships."

It did not happen immediately; *Monitor*-class iron hulls were not very seaworthy. (*Monitor* sank in late 1862 while being towed during a storm off Cape Hatteras.) Wooden ships under both sail and steam power continued to fight the Civil War's deepwater battles, but Dahlgren's words came true after the war. The evolving iron, and then steel, warship incorporated elements from both ironclads: the deeper hull and superstructure of *Virginia* and, rather than multiple-gun broadsides, a few large guns in revolving *Monitor*-type turrets that allowed the guns to be trained without turning the entire vessel.

Only four monitors were built by navy shipyards, but officers considered them the best produced during the war. *Monadnock*, a double-turreted monitor built at Charlestown, was generally thought the best of the lot and the only one of this class to see action. After the war, it proved its unusual seaworthiness by voyaging around Cape Horn to San Francisco.

Other than *Monadnock*, ironcladding work at the Charlestown yard was performed on vessels built elsewhere, although the workers clad with iron the bulwarks of some of the double-ended sidewheelers built there. These vessels, a temporary reprieve for naval sidewheel technology, were designed for the narrow, shallow rivers of the South, allowing the "brown-water" Navy to reverse direction without turning around. The Charlestown yard built five double-enders—the biggest class constructed there during the war and, with those built at other yards, the biggest class of ships produced in the United States before World War I.

The Charlestown yard had in 1858 initiated its first machinist apprenticeship, acknowledging the inevitable transformation of the yard's work. Steam had somewhat prepared the way for the yard's artisans to work with iron: those already trained as boilermakers could adapt their skills to ironcladding. But increasingly the trades related to steam machinery and ironcladding were formalized with titles and apprenticeships. Through the 1850s and '60s, machinists, iron moulders, and boilermakers accounted for an increasingly large part of the workforce: from a total of 26 (3 percent) in 1854 to 371 (19 percent) in 1866. But even though such trades were necessary in the yard by the mid-1860s, they were still in the minority and were paid less, considered less exacting and more easily mastered than the old wooden ship trades.

Samuel Cochran, a longtime employee at Charlestown, recalled later in life that when he arrived at the yard as a young man during the Civil War "the majority of the men employed were ship carpenters and joiners and most of the tools they used were cross cut saws and axes." His own job was to turn the grindstone on which they were sharpened.

Cochran went on to paint a vivid picture of the yard during the war years when some 3,000 workers held jobs there: the ordnance workers who had the dangerous job of retrieving powder from the magazine, donning canvas slippers to reduce the chance of sparks; the clandestine barrels of liquor in cellars, complete with drinking straws; the yard "politicians" who owed their jobs to patronage; sawyers in their six-foot-deep sawpits; the sailors ("Jackies") on the receiving ships finding new ways to get extra grog on board.

A minor labor grievance in 1861 illustrates how the exigencies of war changed the working atmosphere at the yard and reduced the workers' leverage. As it had in 1852, the government decided that yard employees should work sunrise to sunset from September to March, thus bringing their hours in line with those of private yard workers. Again the workers protested, although they continued to work, stating in their petition that they had no desire to hinder the government's campaign to "crush out a foul rebellion." This time the Navy made no concessions. Two strikes in 1862 over the same issue were half-hearted and futile; the longer hours remained in effect.

The sense of urgency and focus engendered by war and the accelerated pace of technological change pushed the yard to extraordinary levels of production. So it was not surprising that with the coming of peace the activity here and at other yards fell off. But the drop was precipitous. At war's end, in sheer numbers and in engine technology, the U.S. fleet compared favorably with those of the European powers. In the weeks after Appomattox, however, the fleet shrank dramatically and continued to decline thereafter. In the postwar economic and political climate, the government's priorities shifted. Massive funds were needed for reconstruction of the southern states and for war-deferred developments of the nation's interior. The Navy would have to wait.

European navies, though, were riding the new wave of technology. In the 1870s their warships began to shed their sailing rigs as steam power became routine technology. But in America the old guard reasserted itself in peace, and there was a reaction against steam. After 1869, all naval vessels, steam or not, were required to have "full sail power," and captains were on notice that they would pay for any coal they consumed other than for emergencies. Four-bladed propellers were replaced with two blades to reduce drag when under sail—with a corresponding loss of steaming efficiency.

As the British and European navies rapidly converted to lighter and stronger iron and then steel hulls on their largest ships, virtually all U.S. vessels built in the 1860s and '70s were wooden-hulled (although some of these contained iron bracing). Even as late as 1885, the *Army and Navy Journal* asserted that "a staunch, fast wooden vessel is still the best for cruising purposes." But while woodenhulled U.S. naval vessels were generally acknowledged to be fine examples of their kind, many were well past their prime; *Independence,* for example, flagship of the first Mediterranean squadron, had been a receiving ship at Mare Island Navy Yard in California since 1857.

It was not only romantic tradition that kept naval shipbuilding in its antebellum condition. Burning coal in warships cost money; the wind, if not as dependable, was free. Sails continued to make good sense on long-distance cruises. America still had no foreign coaling stations to support a distant steam fleet, and isolationist sentiment hindered their acquisition.

For the same political and strategic reasons, America's was a cruising navy, made up of ships not intended for naval battle but for scouting, showing the flag, and commerce raiding. Wooden hulls sufficed for such roles. The government and pri-

Top: *Marines guard the entrance to Charlestown Navy Yard in 1874. The gate no longer exists, but the building at right, dating to 1813, still stands.*

Middle: *Workers in the gun park, 1890s, load cannon and cannonballs onto a cart. Dry dock and carpenter shop can be seen in the background.*

Bottom: *A baseball team of yard workers poses for its picture in front of the machine shop, about 1905.*

vate enterprise continued to look inland, and iron was used instead for rails and bridges to speed westward expansion. In any case, American metallurgy lagged behind that of Britain, while diminishing timber supplies made British designers look to alternate hull materials—not the case in the United States.

If the Navy in general and navy yards in particular declined in the 1870s, Charlestown's relative position was strong. From after the war to the early '80s, Charlestown was the second most productive yard after New York. A large number of vessels came to the yard for repair—mostly wooden vessels with steam engines. To service these ships, Charlestown in the 1870s continued to hire more machinists, engineers, boilermakers, and patternmakers while retaining a solid contingent of wooden ship tradesmen.

Few new vessels were launched from any yard in this period. In the last three decades of the century Charlestown constructed three—all in 1874. The screw sloops *Vandalia* and *Adams* were launched on successive days, the latter (constructed at the yard by a private shipbuilder) being the last wooden warship laid down by the Navy. A few months earlier the yard had launched its first iron-hulled vessel, the torpedo ram *Intrepid*. But it was not part of a general transition to iron. The Navy built only four other iron-hulled vessels, none of them major warships. The 1874 launchings at the Charlestown yard reflected the U.S. Navy's lukewarm and indecisive response to changing naval technology.

The yard by 1880 had changed little since the improvements of the '50s. It had greater capacity now with four shiphouses and two building ways, but the physical plant also reflected the technological limbo into which the Navy had settled. There was a coaling wharf to service steamers and a new rolling mill for iron plate. But the large sail loft and wet timber dock were still very much in use, and oxen still pulled the timbers from dock to sawmill.

The dry dock was occupied by *Hartford* in 1879-80. It was receiving new engines after long tours in the 1860s and '70s on Far Eastern stations. Its two-year stay in the dock—longer than normally needed for such a job—testified to the general state of affairs. The shrinking fleet had reduced the work load and slowed the pace at the yard. Under such conditions it was cheaper to use a smaller crew and take longer to do the work.

That the Navy was willing to give this much attention to so honored a ship as *Hartford* is understandable. But it symbolized the fact that it was only putting off the inevitable—modernization. By the early 1880s the U.S. Navy floundered in the wake of Europe's navies—the victim of limited funds, tradition-bound officers, political neglect, and popular indifference. There were but 48 decaying vessels in commission, most at a Civil War or even prewar level of technology. On top of the other problems, the corruption associated with the administration of Ulysses S. Grant had touched the Navy—including the Charlestown yard—in the late 1870s. Here, as at other yards, politicians found jobs for men who were then expected to vote as they were told. It is easy to see why one historian has characterized this period as the "low water mark" of the Navy.

There were rumors of yard closings. Nothing happened immediately, but less and less work came to Charlestown. Then, in 1883, the Navy suspended all repair and construction work at the yard and reduced its role to manufacturing. So began hard times at Charlestown Navy Yard, during which it came perilously close to shutting down altogether.

Before dry docks came into use in the 16th century, the only way to service a ship's hull was to "careen" it—heave it over on its side, still floating *(see pages 6-7)*, or laying in the mud at low tide. It was difficult and time-consuming and put great strain on the hull. The answer was the dry dock. The concept is simple: float the vessel into a three-sided basin, then close the seaward end and remove all the water. The vessel settles on a cradle, its hull accessible. To undock: reflood the basin, open the seaward end and float the vessel out. But the concept's execution required a finely-engineered complex of masonry, engines, pumps, reservoir, tunnels, culverts, valves, and gates—in effect a huge well-coordinated machine. The Charlestown dry dock and the one built concurrently at Norfolk, Va., were the first such naval structures in the country. Six years under construction, the Charlestown dock was inaugurated in 1833 with the docking of *Constitution*. It was 305 feet long (extended in

2. The pumphouse (D), its steam engine driving two pumps in underground wells (E), pumped the water from the dock via the reservoir and sent it through an underground culvert back to the harbor.

Steam windlass

1. After its 1858 launching, U.S.S. *Hartford* is docked for installation of its steam engine. To empty the dock, workers opened the discharge gates (A), releasing water to flow (➡) down discharge culverts (B) (on both sides of dock) to fill the reservoir (C).

1856 to 370 feet and again in 1948 to 398 feet), 60 feet wide, and 30 feet deep—the Navy's largest dry dock until the 1890s. It took the original eight pumps four to five hours to empty the tremendous basin. Other operations were to some extent governed by Boston Harbor's 10-foot tide. After the dock was enlarged the water level did not rise as rapidly as the tide during filling, so it took two high tides to do the job.

For emptying and filling, the caisson was filled with water and sunk in place between grooves in the dock walls. For docking and undocking, the caisson was emptied and floated out of the way on the high tide *(see right)*. It took 24 men working hand pumps for an hour and a half to expel the water from the caisson. The original wooden caisson lasted until 1901, when the steel caisson still in use today was completed.

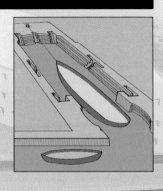

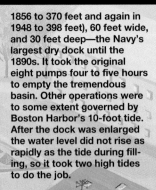

Timber dock

3. To fill the dock, the discharge gates were closed and the filling gates (F) were opened. Water flowed (➡) first to wells (G), then into the dock through the same culverts used to empty it.

Swing gates (backed up caisson)

Caisson ("floating gate")

F

41

The clash of ships at sea embodies the ongoing technological battle between arms and armor: between deploying ever more destructive weapons and contriving ways to withstand them. As long as solid shot was the only way to attack a ship's hull, heavy timbers were usually armor enough. Big wooden warships were rarely sunk by even the heaviest shot. (*Constitution* is a particularly good example.) But the rules of the game changed with the coming of more powerful and more accurate guns, and especially

with the development of the practical explosive shell in the 19th century. A shell could open a gaping hole in a heretofore impervious wooden hull. By 1860 France and then Britain had begun building ironclads. In Britain, especially, the rising cost of diminishing timber supplies was another incentive to experiment with iron, both as armor and for structural elements of the hull. But in the United States, wood was still cheaper than iron. Also, though the country had earlier experimented with ironcladding, the

Navy resisted the new technology, putting emphasis on speed rather than armor. But it quickly made up for lost time after the beginning of the Civil War. The Confederacy took the lead, for the same reason that the United States had built "super-frigates" at the end of the 18th century. A country that could afford only a small navy had to build state-of-the-art warships. The blockade-breaker C.S.S. *Virginia* showed the lethal effectiveness of its ironcladding on its first outing (see page 28). The next day U.S.S. *Monitor*

Inside a Turret

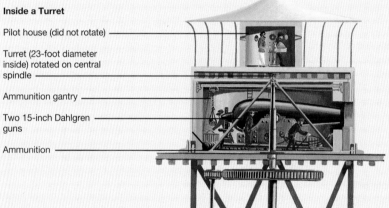

Pilot house (did not rotate)

Turret (23-foot diameter inside) rotated on central spindle

Ammunition gantry

Two 15-inch Dahlgren guns

Ammunition

The monitor Monadnock *(all turreted ironclads were designated monitors) was built at the Charlestown yard in 1862-63. The only monitor built there, it was quite successful, described by Admiral David Dixon Porter as "the best monitor afloat."*

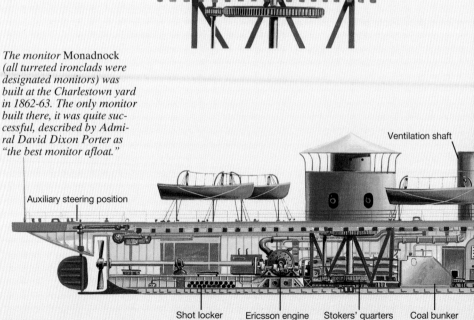

Ventilation shaft

Auxiliary steering position

Shot locker   Ericsson engine   Stokers' quarters   Coal bunker

fought *Virginia* to a draw in the first battle between ironclads *(right)*. The encounter spurred European navies to accelerate their ironclad programs, but new breech-loading rifled guns were demonstrating greater armor-piercing ability. In response iron, and then steel, armor was made thicker and harder, leading to still more powerful guns. The gun designers generally stayed a step ahead, with the biggest guns able to penetrate the thickest armor.

Layers of Protection

1 Typical ironcladding had wooden backing up to three feet thick.

2 A layer of India rubber or felt might be added to help absorb shock and retard corrosion.

3 The cladding was often made up of laminated one-inch iron plates.

4 Tallow was sometimes applied to the outer surface on the theory that it helped deflect shot.

Specifications:

Length overall: 259.5 ft.
Beam (width): 52.5 ft.
Displacement: 3295 tons
Draft: 12 ft., 8 in.
Armor: turrets, 10 in.; pilothouses, 8 in.; over wooden hull, 3-5 in.; deck, 1.5 in.
Engines: Two Ericsson 1426 HP steam engines, 32-in. cylinders; four boilers
Screws: Two 4-bladed screws, 10-ft. diameter
Speed: 9 knots
Crew: 167
Armament: Four 15-in. Dahlgren smoothbore muzzle-loading guns; fired shot or shell

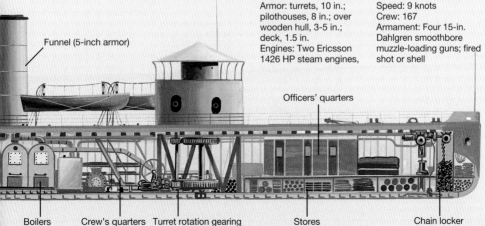

Funnel (5-inch armor)

Officers' quarters

Boilers   Crew's quarters   Turret rotation gearing   Stores   Chain locker

The New Navy

On first looking into the cavernous interior of Shiphouse I, a visitor during the winter of 1884 would have gotten the impression that Charlestown was a busy shipyard. Workers crawled over the almost completed ship-of-the-line *Virginia,* swinging hammers, sawing, pumping hydraulic jacks—apparently applying the finishing touches. But behind the house, growing piles of four-foot lengths of wood told a different story. The workers were breaking up the old 74. *Virginia* had occupied the shiphouse for more than 60 years, through all but the first two of the yard's launchings. Back in 1824, *Virginia* had been within two months of making its own trip down the ways. Now its day had passed, and its great timbers were being reduced to firewood and sold at auction.

Outside the shiphouse, very few workers could have been found among the silent buildings. Charlestown was a moribund yard, barely functioning since its repair and construction duties had been suspended the year before. Only the manufacturing divisions still showed signs of life. In 1886 the yard would be officially converted to a facility that manufactured equipment—especially rope—for vessels built and repaired elsewhere.

The yard was also stripped of much of its equipment and ordered to sell the vessels in ordinary. Repair work fell to an all-time low: between the 1883 docking of the Charlestown-built double-ender *Talapoosa* and 1890, the dry dock was used exactly five times to do repair work for the U.S. Navy—once on the yard tug and four times on the floating gate for the dry dock.

45

Joiner Shop foreman George W. Burroughs, about 1901.
Preceding pages: *Light battleship U.S.S.* Maine *on its first cruise in 1895.* Maine, *part of the new steel navy, blew up in Havana Harbor in 1898 under circumstances still unclear. The resulting Spanish-American War ended Spain's days as a colonial power and made a popular hero of Theodore Roosevelt, who resigned as Assistant Secretary of the Navy to serve in Cuba.*

New construction was out of the question. The yard had known for years that the vessels already in the shiphouses and on the building ways (labeled "Rotten Row" by a local newspaper in 1882) would never be launched. So it came as no surprise that the order closing the yard also condemned *Virginia,* two wooden steamers, and a monitor—the latter three laid down during the Civil War. Still, it was disheartening that in the early 1880s a yard that had built and repaired ships was reduced to taking them apart.

At least the dismantling of vessels provided employment for the workers, who at this point felt quite vulnerable. Throughout the 1880s, "suspension" (being laid off) was always hanging over their heads. More than 500 men were employed at the yard when work was halted in mid-1883. There were around 300 by the end of the year and their ranks continued to thin, averaging less than 200 until 1888—most of them ropemakers, machinists, laborers, and watchmen.

Until World War I, jobs connected with supply would remain more stable than those related to construction and repair. In the late 1880s and '90s, managers found ways to transfer men in the latter trades to other divisions within the yard in order to keep their services on call. But in the early '80s the yard could find virtually no work for men skilled in the craft of wooden shipbuilding—formerly the elite of the workforce. After *Virginia* and the other vessels had been turned into stacks of wood, those who had done the work were sent home.

Now let us look ahead some three decades to 1917, by which time we find a yard dramatically transformed. Eleven wharves described a great arc at the confluence of the Charles and Mystic Rivers. The familiar old shiphouses had been replaced by a large shipbuilding ways and steel plate storage yards. The timber basin that had long dominated the center of the yard was gone, replaced by a new dry dock twice as long as the first one. The other timber basin at the east end of the yard had been filled in and was now the site of gas and oil tanks, a locomotive shed, and a gas plant for acetylene torches.

It was a vital place, showing an intensity not seen since the Civil War. In fact it was again a wartime yard: after almost three years of neutrality the United States had entered the global conflict that was later called World War I. Some 4,500 workers worked two ten-hour shifts or around the clock in three eight-hour shifts, answering to a steam whistle instead of the bell that had summoned 19th-century yard workers. The wharves and docks were crowded with three- and four-stacker steel ships, some carrying the towering cage masts that were a short-lived experiment of the period. On the building ways, workers had laid the keel of the fuel ship *Brazos.*

Electric lights illuminated the thousands of men working on ships through the night. Vessels under repair were alive with the flare of welding torches and the tattoo of pneumatic rivet guns. Over them moved the arms of great cranes, including a 150-ton floating derrick and a colossus that traveled on tracks between dry docks. Materials and equipment were transported by yard locomotives that had replaced the oxen (although horses still did service). A mechanized coaling plant near the old dry dock helped ease the dirty and arduous task of fueling ships. But it was apparently undependable, and at times ships were coaled the old way.

Charlestown's main responsibility was repairing the warships of a greatly enlarged fleet: steel destroyers, armored cruisers and battleships, submarines, and wooden sub chasers. The yard also outfitted and commissioned new vessels, converted civilian vessels to wartime use, armed merchantmen, and altered seized

German passenger liners to transport U.S. troops to France.

More work came to the yard in 1917-18 than in any other comparable period in its history before World War II. Some 450 vessels were serviced during those two years. In addition Charlestown was a supply depot and embarkation point. In all, an average of 50 ships a day arrived at or departed from the yard during the war.

By 1918 some 10,000 skilled workers, laborers, and clericals worked at Charlestown. Reflecting the growth of the labor movement over the last three decades, many of them belonged to trade unions (although they could neither strike nor be represented by the unions in wage negotiations). Women working at the yard were mostly naval yeomen, but a few worked as radio and telephone operators, radio electricians, and ropewalk machine tenders.

Yard employees worked in 17 trade shops, the names of which characterized the needs of modern steel shipbuilding: Shipfitters (including riveters, drillers, welders, sheet metal workers); Electrical; Pattern (for cast metals); Chain; Copper/Pipefitting; and other skills employed in raising a steel ship.

Some of the old familiar shops survived in reduced or altered roles. The sail loft now produced mostly canvas bags, pea jackets, and hammocks. The riggers loft had become a versatile shop responsible for an array of shipyard tasks. They still worked aloft on stacks and steel masts; directed dry docking and crane operations; prepared shipways for launchings; dove beneath ships in hardhat diving suits; and continued to do the traditional rigger's handiwork, such as the braided rope fenders that protected ships' hulls and the fancy leatherwork and ropework still common on naval vessels. The workers in the joiner shop worked on the small wooden boats built at the yard, but spent much of their time making shipboard fur-

Top: *These young women were working as civilian clerks for the Navy when the U.S. entered World War I. Overnight they became Yeomen-F (female) naval personnel. (Yeomen is the naval term for clerical workers.)*

Middle: *Joiners were skilled workers in wood and traditionally the elite of the yard workforce. Even in the early days of steel ships, they remained among the highest paid of the workers. Here joiners are photographed in their shop, about 1897.*

Bottom: *Yard's floating crane, shown here in 1913, could lift 150 tons. Dry Dock 1 is visible in left background.*

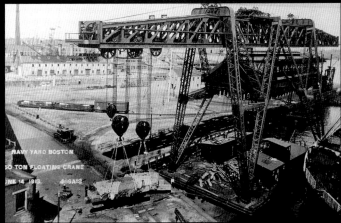

niture. The ropewalk continued to turn out the large quantities of rope still needed on steel ships.

The traditional shipyard hierarchy was virtually unchanged: the crews of mechanics, apprentices, and laborers were headed by leadingmen; several leadingmen were supervised by quartermen; and the quartermen were under a chief quarterman or they answered directly to the master who headed the shop.

Unlike the hard times of the 1880s, the employees at Charlestown had reason to feel secure. Civil Service reforms of the '90s had already gone a long way toward making merit, not political advantage, the criterion for hiring and firing. And now, in the hour of war, the Navy wanted to keep its shipyard workers. In the months before the United States entered the conflict, officials had worried that employees swept up in the popular sentiment for preparedness would enlist. Secretary of the Navy Josephus Daniels declared it the "patriotic duty" of the workers to remain at the yard, asserting that "their services to their country...[are] as important as if they were actually in the field."

When the draft was initiated in 1917, the Navy responded by gaining exemptions for crucial classes of yard workers such as supervisors, draftsmen, and skilled mechanics and their helpers. The military draft gave new meaning to the yard's "six-muster" rule, by which any worker missing six successive roll calls for any reason could be fired. One week after any worker was dismissed, the yard informed his draft board.

The demand for workers and the boosted war economy drove up wages. No doubt prompted by this incentive and by the exemption policy, some 240,000 men applied for work at the yard in 1917-18. But while Charlestown didn't lack for applicants, filling the most skilled positions was a continuing problem. To reme-

dy this (and to help workers gain exemptions), the yard cut a year from the term of apprenticeship and established a trade school to train unskilled workers as mechanics.

While World War I sped up Charlestown's evolution from naval backwater to modern shipyard, other factors had set the process in motion. Time and expected technological advances accounted for some of it. But the transition was accelerated at the yard by a larger transformation of the Navy, prompted by the country's position in a changing world and completed on the stage of the Spanish-American War.

Historians have tagged this transformation the "New Navy." If we simply compare the numbers of the 1880 Navy, when its aging fleet of wooden vessels ranked 12th in the world, to that of the 1900 Navy, when there were in commission or on the stocks 17 steel battleships and a number of armored cruisers, the label "new" is certainly accurate. But there was more to this than simply building new steel ships to catch up to Europe. The Navy's mission underwent a strategic shift in this 20-year period.

The early phase involved a strengthening of the Navy's capacity to carry out its mission. For a century its job had been to defend the shores and to ensure that other navies allowed American merchant vessels free trade anywhere in the world. Its tactical traditions were one-on-one engagements and hit-and-run commerce raiding. But it was clear by the early 1880s that the U.S. Navy was inadequate for even these limited operations. Reformers could point to obvious deficiencies as European navies converted to armored steel hulls in the 1870s and '80s. The old wooden navy had become a disgrace.

Powerful voices were raised in the House Naval Affairs Committee, and in

1883 Congress appropriated money for the steel cruisers *Atlanta, Boston,* and *Chicago,* and the dispatch vessel *Dolphin.* These vessels could still spread a large area of sail, and by European standards were not formidable, but the so-called "ABCD" ships were the core of the New Navy, the first small step towards making the United States a true sea power.

For Charlestown, they were a mixed blessing. The New Navy's need for maintenance and repair bode well for the future, but the immediate effect was devastating. For the same legislation that authorized new ships also established a new criterion for repairing existing vessels. Only repairs that cost less than 30% (later reduced to 20%) of the cost of a new ship of the same size could be performed. This freed up funds to build the new ships, but it also meant so little work for shipyards that both repair and construction work at Charlestown and three other yards was suspended.

In its new role as manufacturing center, the yard kept the ropewalk, rigging loft, and sail loft open. The forge began producing chain and anchors for the new steel ships. But even these activities were sporadic until later in the decade. A survey done one March day in 1884 showed that the ropewalk was spinning rope for *Dolphin*—literally the only thing done that day to help put warships to sea.

During the worst years of the 1880s the ropewalk almost singlehandedly kept the yard alive. It made itself an indispensable facility by supplying virtually all of the Navy's rope. Other shops followed its lead, and by 1890 the Charlestown yard had become an important general manufacturing center, the only naval shipyard producing rope, sail, anchors, and chain. It was still unable to service ships, however. In August 1890 *Chicago* was directed to the yard for repairs, only to turn back because the old dry dock wasn't in good

enough condition to accept the steel cruiser. "Repairs to engine bolts" for *Boston* typified the kind of task the yard could perform.

But 1890 also marked the beginning of the yard's rebirth. Congress appropriated $152,000 for new machine tools and modernization of Charlestown's crumbling facilities. It wasn't enough to remake the yard, but it was a start. It was also the year that Commander Alfred Thayer Mahan, president of the Naval War College and one-time aide to the Charlestown Navy Yard commandant, published *The Influence of Sea Power Upon History, 1660-1783.* This important book helped to stimulate the world-wide buildup of naval forces prior to World War I. His thesis (greatly simplified) was as follows: A combination of geography, population size, and "national character" makes a great seafaring nation. Essential to the continued well-being of such a nation is a government that actively promotes a vigorous maritime commerce. "Sea power"—command of the sea lanes—protects this commerce. Only large concentrated fleets of capital ships able to engage and destroy the enemy's navy can create and maintain sea power.

Mahan's influence, both as author and adviser to the Secretary of the Navy, was pivotal. His writings strengthened the hand of imperialists and reformers who had called for new strategic thinking. The United States, they reasoned, was a growing industrial power with increasing overseas interests, and some—among them Mahan disciple and future Assistant Secretary of the Navy and President Theodore Roosevelt—believed the nation should have a navy befitting its role, one able to open markets, protect those economic interests, and project U.S. power.

In a burst of enthusiasm recalling that for the ship-of-the-line at the end of the War of 1812, Congress in 1890 authorized the country's first full-sized battleships. They represented enormous commitments of resources, time, and money. Called "coastline" battleships to placate still powerful coast defense advocates, they were nevertheless another step in the United States' emergence by the turn of the century as a world power with a widening sphere of influence. The Navy kept its faith in battleships until their vulnerability to air power and the superiority of aircraft carriers as attack weapons were demonstrated in World War II.

Although a succession of battleships, cruisers, submarines, and other vessels were now being laid down, Charlestown didn't immediately reap the benefits. The majority of the warships launched between 1883 and 1905 were built by contract in private yards, and Charlestown built none of them. For most of the 1890s, the yard continued to be primarily a manufacturing facility. The New Navy's hulls did account for much of the yard's repair work. Steel hulls didn't rot, but they more easily fouled with barnacles and seaweed than a coppered wooden hull and were less resistant to corrosion than iron. Maintaining them became the Charlestown yard's bread and butter.

The Spanish-American War broke this pattern, making Charlestown once again a repair yard. Besides the new warships the United States was trying out against the Spanish navy, there was also the "mosquito fleet" (old monitors, converted yachts, and other small craft used for coastal defense during the war) to be maintained and repaired. In all some 50 vessels were serviced by 1,200–1,400 workers.

To beef up its workforce for war, the yard began hiring more foreign workers, especially from Scandinavian countries with shipbuilding traditions. Charlestown thereafter maintained a workforce averaging over 2,000 during the two decades before World War I—compared to the

fewer than 400 workers there through most of the 1890s. The Spanish-American War was pivotal, marking a permanent expansion in the size and diversity of the Charlestown workforce.

At war's end the United States was recognized as a world power with attendant responsibilities. This new status was symbolized by the establishment of a coaling station in the recently acquired Philippines. The capital ship building program continued apace—given renewed vigor by President Theodore Roosevelt, staunch advocate of big ships and a strong navy.

The yard continued to be mainly a repair facility with a steadily increasing workload. The new 750-foot Dry Dock 2, authorized three months after the sinking of *Maine,* was built to receive the Navy's biggest ships. But soon after the massive structure's 1905 completion, Britain launched H.M.S. *Dreadnought,* ushering in an even larger class of battleship the dock could not accommodate.

In this period the yard specialized in the smaller battleships and the newest type of warship: destroyers. These fast, versatile ships had evolved from British "torpedo boat destroyers" built in the 1880s to counter the new torpedo boats. The mobile torpedo, also developed in Britain, was a self-propelled explosive device launched from a warship's deck, traveling underwater to open the hull of its target.

Developments in naval technology from the 1880s to the eve of World War II included nothing quite so dramatic as the epochal shifts from sail to steam and wood to iron, but the period saw advances in strategic weapons such as submarines and aircraft carriers, and major innovations that resulted in ships and shipbuilding essentially like what we see today. In the period before the age of flight, sophisticated warships were highly visible embodiments of the state of a nation's

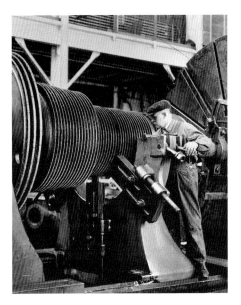

Lathe operator shapes steam turbine rotor for destroyer tender Whitney *in 1923.*
Preceding pages: *Charlestown's machine shop in 1913. Overhead belts transferred power from a central steam engine to the machines. The potentially hazardous belts were later replaced with electric motors on each machine.*

technology, and the rapidly expanding U.S. fleet was an unmistakable sign of its growing industrial and technological prominence.

The major innovations were again in hull material and propulsion. The transition from iron to steel hulls further liberated naval engineers. Lighter, stronger, and less brittle, steel allowed them more play in hull size and proportions. Despite extensive use of ironclads by the United States during the Civil War, its navy essentially skipped the iron stage in seagoing warships, moving from *Hartford*-type wooden steamers to the steel ABCD ships of 1883. While the Charlestown yard launched no steel warships until the 1930s, it did construct the tug *Pentucket* (1903) and training bark *Cumberland* (1904), both steel-hulled.

As steam engines grew more efficient in the 1880s and '90s, sailing rigs were made smaller and vestigial masts served mainly as radio antennae and platforms for directing big guns. But a revolution in steam technology sent reciprocating engines the way of masts on most large naval vessels. Steam turbines, which were much more efficient at sustained high speeds, were developed in the 1880s in Europe and used in 1905 on *Dreadnought*. In America they became truly practical during the World War I period.

Along with the introduction of turbines came an innovation in the fuel that powered them. During the 1890s oil was introduced, used in combination with coal. By 1910 the United States had built its first all oil-burning warship. Besides providing greater power more quickly, oil needed less storage space and fewer engine room hands than coal.

These advances and refinements completed the evolution of the U.S. Navy warship from wooden-hulled sailing vessel to powered steel ship. But perfecting the new technology was not the only challenge associated with the transition. The demands of modern naval design provoked growing controversy over how work should be performed at naval shipyards and how those yards should be organized. Charlestown Navy Yard played a central role in the debate.

Since 1868 the nation's naval shipyards had each been organized into departments corresponding to those at the Navy Department level. Each department head, though nominally under the yard commandant, really worked for his boss in Washington. So each department became in effect a separate plant protecting its own interests and budget. When a yard built relatively simple wooden-hulled ships powered by steam engines, the tasks of the Construction and Steam Engineering departments differed enough that there was little overlap. The old organization was not then a problem. But as warships became complex, integrated machines the system broke down, providing little coordination between departments and a great deal of duplication. By 1910 it was grossly wasteful and inefficient, a public scandal.

At about the same time as reformers were calling for a shakeup of naval shipyards, the phrase "scientific management" was being bandied about. Everyone recognized that the 19th-century industrial system, while highly successful, had to be managed differently to best incorporate 20th-century technology. The most famous of the new management systems was that of Frederick Winslow Taylor. Taylor's system called for the strict application of scientific methods to industrial management and organization in order to produce the maximum output. Specifically, efficiency experts would study workers' tasks and break them down into their smallest components; perform time-and-motion studies to eliminate wasteful motions and determine the

optimum time in which a task should be completed; and offer wage incentives and penalties for meeting or falling short of the new standards. There would be no reason for bargaining or for unions since non-debatable scientific principles, rather than human foibles and emotions, would govern management decisions.

The workers' response to Taylorism was speedy and unequivocal. They fiercely resisted any system that would analyze their movements as if they were machines to be fine-tuned (not an exaggeration of Taylor's stated beliefs). Such a system, they said, would demean them and their skills—robbing them of their autonomy and individuality; eliminating craft from the job; turning workers into mere cogs performing sped-up, repetitive tasks "to the physical breaking point"—not to mention the threat to collective bargaining. So visceral was their reaction to Taylorism that any kind of management system became suspect.

Thus when the Navy attempted in 1912 to introduce a British management system—less doctrinaire than Taylorism, though with the same ends of efficiency and increased production—workers at Charlestown were immediately on their guard. The system's reorganization of the yard's divisions also upset established power relationships between traditional sea (line) officers and newer and often younger engineering (staff) types, tilting the balance in favor of the latter. Not surprisingly, line and staff were polarized over the merits of the new order, accusing each other respectively of obstructing progress and overmanaging.

In this charged atmosphere, when two overzealous junior officers attempted to introduce minute Taylor-like task breakdowns at Charlestown, the metal workers at the yard took action. They asked their congressman to hand-deliver a protest to Assistant Secretary of the Navy Franklin

Top: *Machine shop workers pose for a group picture in Dry Dock 1, about 1905. At this time a little more than 2,000 employees worked at the Charlestown yard.*

Bottom: *U.S.S. Whitney rises amid a forest of scaffolding. The keel of the 484-foot destroyer tender—the largest vessel ever built at Charlestown—was laid down in 1921. It took two and a half years to build. After surviving the Japanese attack on Pearl Harbor,* Whitney served in the Pacific during World War II.

D. Roosevelt. While Roosevelt agreed in principle with scientific management, he was generally sympathetic to labor and refused to implement a system that the yard workers opposed.

Roosevelt's visit to the yard in 1913, during which he let it be known that certain junior officers were being reassigned, focused national attention on the controversy and encouraged other yard workers around the nation. A delegation representing them lobbied against Taylorism, eventually persuading Congress to outlaw such management systems in navy yards. Yet when it was all over, the Charlestown yard was organized quite differently than in the 19th century, making it a more efficient builder and repairer of modern naval vessels and helping it to perform as it did during World War I.

U.S.S. *Bridge,* commissioned as the first American troops were enroute to France, exemplified the yard's progress since the dark 1880s. Following a long campaign by a job-desperate Boston to have the ship built at Charlestown, *Bridge* was laid down in 1914 and launched two years later. It was the Navy's first refrigerated supply ship, with a steel hull and a boiler that could burn oil or coal. Its 423-foot length made *Bridge* the largest vessel yet built at Charlestown and its first major ship since the 1870s.

After demonstrating its competence with *Bridge,* Charlestown was assigned *Brazos,* two other fuel ships, and a destroyer tender. The war-spurred building program helped Charlestown stay busy when peace came, as the last three vessels weren't laid down until after the armistice. In fact the number of employees actually rose, to almost 13,000 in 1919. Besides the shipbuilding, there was work converting ships to troop transports to bring the soldiers home and stripping military gear from ships returning to civilian service. Charlestown repaired a large

number of destroyers, subs, and battleships small enough for Dry Dock 2. To increase its docking capacity, the yard purchased in 1920 a new state-built dry dock in South Boston. At the time it was the country's largest dry dock, becoming the nucleus of the yard's South Boston Annex.

Events conspired in the 1920s to dampen the yard's postwar prosperity. The 1922 Five-Power Treaty limited new ship construction and the overall number of vessels, meaning less repair and outfitting work for naval shipyards. In any case the political mood was to spend money on other things. After the destroyer tender *Whitney* was launched in 1923, there was no more construction at Charlestown, other than a couple of tugs, for the rest of the decade. And as the Japanese grew increasingly expansionist, much of the fleet was moved to the West Coast, further reducing work at the yard.

Nevertheless, Charlestown kept up its steady repair work, especially on destroyers, albeit at a more modest level and with a workforce reduced to below 3,000 by 1922. The addition of a marine railway in 1919 allowed the yard to more easily service smaller ships of up to 2,000 tons.

By the end of the decade further developments seriously threatened the Charlestown yard. The London Naval Treaty of 1930 extended the moratorium on new capital ship construction for another six years. The treaty further required the U.S. to scrap three battleships and 94 destroyers—the latter a mainstay of Charlestown. The deepening Depression also hurt the yard, as the government's austerity program in the early years of the crisis reduced work at naval shipyards. The Hoover administration threatened to close most federal yards, including Charlestown. Yet in the Depression itself we can trace the roots of the coming boom.

Building a Steel Ship

Beginning in the 1880s, steel rapidly supplanted wood as the primary material in U.S. naval vessels. Charlestown began building large steel vessels in 1915-20, the period depicted below. Stronger per pound than wood or iron, steel enabled naval architects to design bigger ships that could carry more armament. Steel was also better suited to bearing the massive weight of steam engines and boilers. The structural members of early steel vessels were riveted together, with limited gas welding in use by World War I.

Shipyard artisans traded auger, saw, and mallet for pneumatic drill, gas cutting torch, and pneumatic rivet gun. Massive steam-powered cranes replaced the old hoisting shears. Yet, while a riveted steel ship demanded vastly more complicated plans and

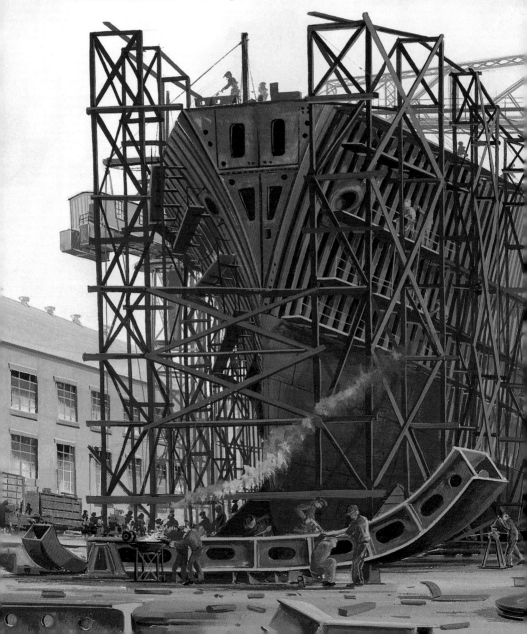

a higher level of coordination between shops, it was assembled in much the same way as a wooden vessel. From the keel rose the stem, sternpost, and frames. Transverse beams, longitudinals, vertical stanchions, watertight bulkheads, decking, and plating completed the hull, all held together by rivets. Electric welding *(right)*, developed in the 1930s, allowed still lighter construction and the prefabrication of sections. Designers, however, still called for rivets for some parts of the hull throughout World War II.

When the Charlestown yard began constructing steel ships in 1915, a new building ways was erected on the site of the shiphouse in which the wooden screw frigate **Merrimack** *had been built 60 years earlier (see pages 32-33). The yard built three 475-foot fuel ships ("oilers") on this shipways between 1917 and 1921, reducing the time between keel laying and launch from two years for the first ship to less than a year for the last.*

Chain for the Navy

Until World War I, forged iron chain was used on naval vessels, and the forge shop at the Charlestown yard was a leader in the industry. But it was a laborious process, and the demands of war spurred the development of cast steel chain, which could be produced more quickly. Charlestown was soon experimenting with detachable links to connect standard chain lengths. This led to the development in 1926 of a new chainmaking process, in which each link was made from half-links joined in a die under a drop-forge hammer—"die-lock" chain. It was clearly superior: more uniform, stronger, cheaper to make. By the early 1930s Charlestown was producing die-lock chain in several sizes, and by 1936 die-lock had superseded cast steel chain for all sizes. The shop made the chain used in most U.S. naval vessels built during World War II and was the only forge to make chain for the largest postwar aircraft carriers. (*Right*) Finished chain is loaded for shipping.

The Die-lock Chainmaking Process

1 Rolled nickel-steel rods (from ¾-inch to 4¾-inch in diameter) are cut into shorter bars.

2 The cut bars are heated in a gas furnace to 2100°F. The now-malleable bars are bent by machine into U-shapes.

3 The U-bars are stamped to form stems, with tapered and ridged ends, or they have holes punched in the ends to form sockets.

4 Stem is hooked onto last completed link and placed in die; socket is heated, and the two are joined under a 10,000-pound hammer *(opposite page)*.

5 Largest 4¾-inch chain for supercarriers could withstand up to 2.5 million pounds. Each two-foot-long link weighed 360 pounds. Red undercoat and grey paint helped retard rusting.

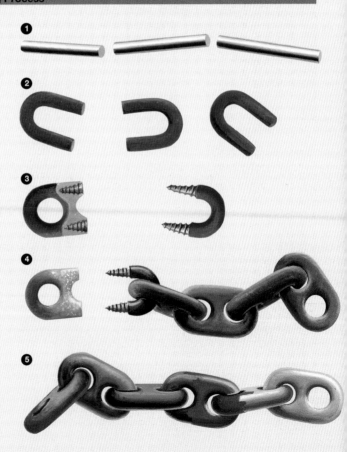

61

The Yard Transformed

It was not a dramatic launch—no gathering speed down the shipways and plunging into Boston Harbor. Instead, the water flowing into Dry Dock 1 rose slowly around U.S.S. *MacDonough* until the destroyer lifted off the keel blocks and was towed out of the dock. The 1934 "floating" was low-keyed but significant. *MacDonough* was the first warship built by Charlestown since the wooden screw sloop *Vandalia* slid down the ways in 1874.

The technological leap between the two vessels—partially bridged by the steel supply and fuel ships Charlestown built in the World War I period—was considerable. Except for its coal-fired auxiliary steam propulsion, the 216-foot *Vandalia* did not differ significantly from the old *Constitution*. *MacDonough* was a modern destroyer—the sloop-of-war's 20th-century counterpart—incorporating the advances of the past 60 years. It was powered by geared turbines driven by steam generated in oil-burning boilers, and relied on sophisticated electrical, hydraulic, and communications systems. At 341 feet, its steel hull took up most of Dry Dock 1.

As soon as *MacDonough* was moved out of the dock, the destroyer *Monaghan,* just floated from Dry Dock 2, was moved into #1 for completion and outfitting. Two more keels were immediately laid in #2. It is noteworthy that neither dry dock was being used to repair ships. In fact, the whole yard's traditional role as repair facility had given way in the past year to a new one as shipbuilder, a status it maintained through World War II. Charlestown built 12 destroyers in the 1930s and 24 more by

Navy Yard Complex During World War II

Chelsea Naval Hospital

CHELSEA

MYSTIC RIVER

CHARLESTOWN

Chelsea Naval Annex

CHELSEA RIVER

Fuel Depot Annex

Navy Yard

EAST BOSTON

Pipeline

CHARLES RIVER

East Boston Annex

DOWNTOWN BOSTON

BOSTON HARBOR

Deep Water Pier

South Boston Annex

SOUTH BOSTON

This map of Boston Harbor in 1942 shows the five units of Charlestown Navy Yard during World War II. By war's end the South Boston Annex was the largest, with dry docks big enough to repair battleships and heavy cruisers. The Chelsea and East Boston Annexes repaired small vessels, and the Fuel Depot Annex served the great number of naval vessels entering the harbor during the war.
Preceding pages: *At a shift change in 1943, departing workers hurry past destroyer escorts being outfitted for war. At its peak during the war, the Charlestown yard and its annexes employed more than 50,000 men and women.*

the end of the war. Of course the yard built and serviced other types of vessels—especially destroyer escorts and LSTs (Landing Ship Tank)—but Charlestown acquired a reputation as a "destroyer yard" and thereafter specialized in this workhorse of the Navy.

Ironically, the change had been brought about by the same economic crisis that almost put an end to the yard. After considering closing all yards but Norfolk and Philadelphia to save money, the Hoover administration in 1931 proposed closing only the Charlestown yard. Reaction was swift: committees were formed in Boston; petitions protesting the closing were signed. But it was probably the fact that *MacDonough* had been ordered a month earlier that tilted the scales in the yard's favor. The keel was not laid for two years, however, and 1932 was the yard's bleakest year since before the Spanish-American War, with only 1,500 people employed.

The Roosevelt administration's program to stimulate the economy, provide jobs, and pull the nation out of the Depression was the first step in Charlestown's transformation into a true ship construction yard. Under FDR's 1933 National Industrial Recovery Act, 32 new warships were authorized, 20 of them destroyers, of which two were assigned to Charlestown. The following year, growing worries about Japanese aggression moved Congress to further expand the Navy.

The yard kept a rapid pace in the 1930s, laying two keels simultaneously in Dry Dock 2 in 1934 and again in 1935. (As the shipways was inadequate for destroyers, all keels were laid in this dock until 1939.) After floating, the hulls were moved into Dry Dock 1 for completion, the whole process taking about two years.

Repair work was much reduced in the 1930s by federal economy measures specifying lengthened maintenance intervals. As both dry docks were in any case usually tied up in construction work, and because most of the ships in for repair were relatively small, many of these vessels were floated into a large cradle and hauled from the water up the tracks of the yard's marine railway. Others were taken across the harbor to the South Boston dry dock.

Technological change transformed many of the yard's oldest trades by the 1930s, while the growing size and complexity of ships required more and more workers. Such large government employers as shipyards were seen by policy makers as places to both promote economic stability and save money. Early in the Depression these two goals were addressed, respectively, with lower and upper limits for each yard's workforce—at Charlestown, 1,500 and 1,800. The workforce stayed generally within these limits until 1935, when it began growing, reaching some 5,000 workers by late 1939. (During hard times the yard kept its eye on the future, exempting apprentices from layoffs.)

By the time war had begun in Europe in 1939, with "readiness" again America's watchword, the yard was operating at an even faster rate of production than in the mid-thirties. With the shipways enlarged to handle destroyers, six ships were in some stage of construction that summer. In October four destroyers were floated out of Dry Dock 2 on the same day. The yard also prepared 18 of the old World War I four-stacker destroyers for transfer to Britain under the 1940 destroyers-for-bases agreement.

Then came the war. If the thirties had been a period of gearing up, wartime pushed the yard into overdrive. It took a great war effort for the yard to realize its true shipbuilding and manufacturing potential, confirming a statement by Secretary of the Navy George von Meyer in 1910: "Navy yards are primarily for war and only incidentally for peace." One his-

torian's conservative estimate: under the goad of war the yard built, repaired, overhauled, converted, or outfitted some 6,000 vessels between 1939 and 1945.

The raid on Pearl Harbor in December 1941 made every naval installation fearful of enemy attacks. Charlestown installed anti-aircraft batteries on roofs and camouflaged waterfront buildings. Some security measures were disruptive of yard routine. Blackouts and dim-outs were in force, especially in the early years of the war, to reduce the chances of ships being silhouetted against lights. When the air raid whistle blew, workers had to stop what they were doing and go to shelters. Throughout the war, yard officials juggled the conflicting demands of security and production.

Other security measures had more personal consequences. Some yard workers were banned from certain areas, and everyone was forbidden to speak foreign languages while at work. A number of workers were suspended in 1941 as security risks. "Remarks...inimical to the government" were enough to earn an employee a place on the suspension list.

The huge number of people working at Charlestown was another sign that the yard had been remade by war. The U.S. Navy became the world's largest single employer of industrial labor during the conflict, and the Charlestown yard held the same status in the Boston area. The yard's force rapidly swelled from 5,000 workers in 1939 to a high of about 50,000 at Charlestown and its annexes in mid-1943, working around the clock in three eight-hour shifts.

As in World War I, the yard again had to protect its essential employees from the draft board. But voluntary enlistment proved to be the real drain on the workforce. Although yard foremen tried to dissuade crucial employees from going, some 13,000 workers left the yard to join the fight. Throughout the conflict, even when

After the construction boom created by World War II, Charlestown resumed its traditional role of "serving the fleet" (the yard's motto). In the early 1950s it was the home yard for 121 vessels, including U.S.S. *Cassin Young*, the destroyer now on exhibit at the yard. All types of ships, but especially destroyers, came for everything from minor repairs to overhauls on established cycles. The latter, which often involved some degree of modernization, could require 800 to 900 workers a day. After the war the yard preserved decommissioned vessels of the Atlantic Reserve Fleet berthed at the South Boston Annex. Charlestown also prepared ships for transfer to allies, outfitted vessels built elsewhere, and repaired equipment, especially sonar.

Charlestown was busy in 1960 with overhauls and modernizations. In the foreground: aircraft carrier Wasp *(whose crew presented the yard with the plaque shown above); floating dry dock (in a yard dry dock); heavy cruiser* Macon *(CA-132).*

more than 50,000 people worked there, the yard was shorthanded.

To make up for the shortages, the yard began for the first time hiring significant numbers of women and African Americans. Their door of opportunity, unlocked by the needs of a war economy, was kept open by pressure from civil rights groups on the Roosevelt administration (often relayed by a sympathetic Eleanor Roosevelt). Women at the yard had traditionally worked in clerical positions and as phone operators, and this remained true at war's outset. But more and more women found work in the industrial shops, notably as welders and at the ropewalk (the latter having employed them during World War I). At least in some shops, however, there were restrictions. Gloria Brandenberg, who worked in the Paint Shop, recalled that all painter's helpers were female, supervised by a woman (the "leading lady"), while all painters were male. Brandenberg said there was no chance for advancement.

By 1943 female blue-collar workers outnumbered women in clerical positions. Some 7,700 women were on the rolls in late 1944—far above their prewar level and about 19 percent of the workforce. Many worked as welders on ships under construction, but yard officials wary of contact between female workers and male crews barred women from all vessels in for repair. Painter's helper Brandenberg recalled that the women were not allowed even to talk to sailors.

While African Americans were not officially excluded from Charlestown's prewar workforce, few had been employed. When the war created opportunities for them, some whites openly resisted their presence in skilled positions. But this was not a universal attitude. Allan Crite, a black illustrator in the Design Department, said he experienced no racial problems. Inevitably, though, tensions arose in some areas. Gloria Brandenberg recalled an evening at a social club with her coworkers from the Paint Shop, one of whom was African American. She was asked to leave. The group talked it over; they all left. But the records show no major racial conflict at the yard. At war's end more than 2,300 African Americans were in the force of 32,000 workers.

By late 1942, the yard had settled into a wartime routine—to the extent that routine is possible during war. Normal peacetime constraints didn't apply. "During the war there wasn't much emphasis on estimates," recalled plumber Lyman Carlow. "For one thing, there wasn't time. Here's the job; we need the ship right away; get it done and whatever it costs it costs…it was just a real frantic pace…the material just flowed in…plenty of people, so we could really get the work done."

More than the higher level of general activity and the large numbers of workers (around 36,000 at this point), it was the volume of new construction that characterized the wartime yard. A walk around the yard on November 23 would have revealed ships being built in every facility but Dry Dock 2, used only for repairs.

Workers generally laid down and launched large vessels in pairs. But while floating two at a time out of a dry dock was standard practice, it was never approached casually. John Langan, a shipfitter during the war, recalled: "It was quite a feat, two destroyers right alongside each other, flooding the dock, and not having them crash."

A new shipways built in early 1941 helped quicken the pace of production. In that year 10 destroyers were laid down, the most in any one year. By late 1941 the yard's workers had pushed the time for building a destroyer down to a little over a year and would cut it to three or four months from keel to launching by the end of the war.

"We all felt that we were doing our job, and the harder we worked, the faster we would get the ships out and the faster it would get over. Deep down, everyone was very serious about it, because ninety-nine out of a hundred people had a husband or a brother or somebody close to them that was overseas."

— *Gloria Brandenberg, WW II*
Charlestown yard worker

As enlistments and competition from private industry depleted the pool of male workers during World War II, the Navy looked to the large numbers of women who wanted to do their part for the war effort. Women had long worked at the Charlestown yard, although almost exclusively (except during World War I) in clerical positions. But beginning in 1942 the easing of state workweek restrictions for women hastened their recruitment into the yard's manufacturing and traditional shipyard shops. The intention was to have them replace men in relatively unskilled positions requiring little training. And in fact most women did work as helpers in their shops, often with little chance of advancement. But some moved into the trades as machinists, riveters, painters, riggers, pipefitters, and especially as welders and ropewalk workers. At the same time women still occupied more than half of the yard's clerical positions. Altogether, they made up about one-fifth of the yard workforce by 1945. Those in the trades knew their jobs would likely end when the war did, but the point had been made. In 1945, a yard historian wrote: "Experience over the past two years has proven that female employees are able to work efficiently on an equal basis with men on many jobs that were formerly considered to be men's jobs."

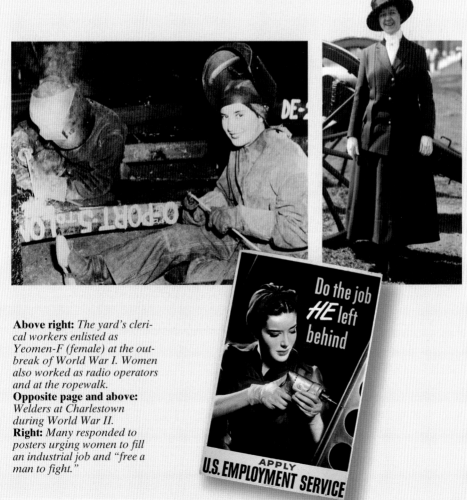

Above right: *The yard's clerical workers enlisted as Yeomen-F (female) at the outbreak of World War I. Women also worked as radio operators and at the ropewalk.*
Opposite page and above: *Welders at Charlestown during World War II.*
Right: *Many responded to posters urging women to fill an industrial job and "free a man to fight."*

Do the job *HE* left behind

APPLY
U.S. EMPLOYMENT SERVICE

The new shipways was also used to build destroyer escorts (DEs)—smaller, slower, and less expensive versions of destroyers designed for escort duty and antisubmarine warfare. Escorted convoys had proven to be the only effective way to thwart U-boat "wolf packs" preying on allied shipping. In 1942, after the Navy ordered the first of more than a thousand DEs, Charlestown built a new dry dock in which it could turn out four at a time. The next year 50 DEs were laid down at the yard, half of which were destined for Britain in accordance with the Lend-Lease Act of 1941. Charlestown got the production of DEs down to an art: of the 62 it built, workers launched an impressive 46 in the first eleven months of 1943.

If 1941 was the year of the destroyer at the yard and 1943 belonged to the DE, 1944 was the year of the LST (Landing Ship, Tank). These seagoing assault vessels carried tanks and other vehicles during amphibious landings. The yard laid down 30 in 1944, taking only a month to complete one of the 328-foot vessels.

In all, Charlestown built 174 large vessels during the war, including 12 barracks ships and four submarines. There were also hundreds of smaller craft, such as wooden motor launches and diver boats. The South Boston Annex played a part in the yard's strong wartime performance, doing much of the repair and conversion work and fabricating hull sections that were towed to Charlestown for incorporation into ships under construction.

Not all vessels were built outside: in the summer of 1942, shipfitters fabricated in their shop 150 fifty-foot LCMs (Landing Craft, Mechanized)—also called "tank lighters"—for the British-American invasion of North Africa. Shipfitter John Langan remembered it as a "crash program... We just stopped everything else and concentrated on them and delivered them for the invasion."

While this kind of rapid, assembly-line construction was Charlestown's specialty during the war, there were other claims on the yard's time. By late 1942 war's reality was being brought home to Charlestown in the shape of battle-scarred ships needing quick repair. When a damaged ship arrived, it was given priority until it was ready to return to combat.

There was another reason for the air of urgency around war repairs: ship repair generally called for more skill than did shipbuilding. Because workers often had to work blind on battle damage until its nature and extent could be determined, such work called on all the workers' resourcefulness. John Langan remembered "everybody fighting to get them [war-damaged vessels], because it is good work." Langan recalled one vessel towed into the yard: it had been "torpedoed and cut right in halves...and the fireroom was open to the seas...[They had] tied her down with big I-beams...tied them the full length, all the way around"—to keep the ship afloat until it reached the yard.

Even without the shell-torn hulls and shredded superstructures, war is hard on ships. Pushed faster, farther, and longer under less than ideal conditions, they needed more than routine maintenance. And on top of the already demanding schedule of ship construction, repair, and maintenance, other tasks competed for time and resources. Yard workers outfitted naval vessels built at other yards. They converted private vessels and old naval ships to wartime uses. They manufactured turbines and thousands of tons of die-lock chain *(see pages 60-61)*. They "degaussed" hulls—neutralized their magnetic fields so they would not trip mines. Together these activities suggest the scope and grueling pace of the yard's war effort.

In such an atmosphere, mishaps caused by fallible humans dealing with complex machinery were inevitable. One particularly embarrassing, and nearly tragic, incident was related by electrical shop foreman Mel Hooper. His men were completing electrical work on the new submarine *Lancefish* (built at another yard) in 1945. "Some machinist went down," he recalled, "and opened up the front gate on the torpedo tube and forgot to close it; then he went back in the ship and opened up the inside one and then it started to flood. And they had a hell of a job trying to close it, and they couldn't close it, and everybody ran aboard the dock to get the hell out of there before they got drowned. And then the ship sank."

The stepped-up safety program was almost certainly an improvement on the pre-war conditions, when, as remembered by plumber Lyman Carlow, "It seemed to me that everyone was supposed to look after himself." But while the program called for more protections for workers from open machinery, hazardous fumes, and other dangerous conditions, a survey in 1944 noted that workers were rarely disciplined for safety violations, machines lacked guards, and most workers did not wear their hard hats, goggles, or ear protection. "You [went] down to the tanks with the chipping hammers and riveting guns going all around," recalled Carlow, "and you wouldn't be able to hear for a couple of hours afterward. But nobody did anything about it, or thought anything of it. You just got deaf, and that was it."

A shipyard was a dangerous place to work even in peacetime; war multiplied the hazards. Charles Snell, an apprentice rigger at the yard, recalled 40 years later, "We had a lot of close escapes, because safety wasn't really stressed then as much as it is today...we lost a lot of riggers, strangely enough, and I can never account for this, being run over by the cranes...the operator of the crane, when it was traveling, had very limited visibility close ahead. And we lost an inordinate number of riggers because they'd stumble and the crane would run over them....We had quite a few falls into the dry dock, not riggers, but all trades."

Snell left the yard in 1943 and served in Europe for the duration of the war. He recalled his impressions upon returning in 1946, comparing the yard to "a runner, which was running for an objective, and all of a sudden, the objective wasn't there. The need for everything had suddenly evaporated. And it was a question of what do you finish and what don't you finish, and what's important."

With peace came the end of Charlestown's brief period as a major shipbuilding center. But the war-seasoned yard did not simply revert to what it had been before. Charlestown found a new postwar role as a place where old vessels were remade from the inside out, transformed into modern warships. Old did not necessarily mean long in years. In the 1950s, ships that had performed admirably in the late war were being left behind in a world of accelerating technological change. Charlestown extended their careers, installing state-of-the-art electronics. When advances in missile technology opened a new era in naval weapons and strategy, Charlestown played a leading role in the changeover. The life of the crowded and aging yard itself was extended by such activities, enabling Charlestown to render another three decades of service to the country.

In the months after war's end, the level of activity naturally fell off, but the yard remained busy converting transports to bring home the troops, inactivating ships, and completing the last few LSTs, barracks ships, and subs laid down in 1945. Charlestown also carved a niche for itself in sonar, a technology dating to the World War I period and considered standard equipment since the 1930s. Beginning in 1948 the yard became a center for the repair of sonar equipment, establishing a sonar laboratory and developing techniques adopted by other electronics repair centers throughout the Navy.

Radar, developed in the 1930s, had come into widespread use during the war. The yard undertook a major conversion program in 1950 when it began upgrading radar and sonar systems on a number of destroyers and destroyer escorts, converting them to radar picket and antisubmarine warfare (ASW) roles. Charlestown also planned and designed all alterations, wherever they were performed, to cruisers, destroyers, escort carriers, LSTs, and several auxiliary vessel types.

While the yard accepted a variety of vessels, including aircraft carriers, it continued its traditional specialization in destroyers and destroyer escorts. In 1955 the yard converted the 10-year-old *Gyatt* into the world's first guided missile destroyer.

That year the yard laid down the keel of its only postwar vessel and the last one it built: the LST *Suffolk County*, first of a larger and faster class of LSTs. Charlestown also served as the design yard for the other six LSTs, built in private yards.

In the 1960s the yard stayed busy with outfittings, missile and ASW conversions, and Fleet Rehabilitation and Modernization (FRAM) overhauls that added five to seven years of service to aging warships. Charlestown's FRAM program specialized in World War II-era destroyers. Ranging from brief dockings to major operations of a year or more costing millions, these projects involved such sophisticated work as installing or upgrading sonar *(see pages 76-77)*, radar, communications, and computer equipment; major alterations such as replacing engines and entire superstructures; and the more prosaic tasks the yard had been performing for over a century: cleaning and painting hulls, renovating propellers and rudders, and rebricking or replacing boilers.

Nevertheless, by 1972 work was falling off at Charlestown, and signs did not bode well for the yard's future. For years the Navy had invested little there for maintenance or modernization, making it harder to stay efficient. The marine railway and ropewalk had been shut down in 1971. Elsewhere, superfluous or inefficient military bases were being closed to save money. (The New York Navy Yard was closed in 1966.) A massive infusion of funds was needed to upgrade the old Charlestown yard—too small in any case for proper expansion of its facilities.

The Navy in general was retrenching for economic reasons. The destroyer fleet, especially—the lifeblood of the yard in the 20th century—had steadily dwindled since 1960. The fewer destroyers there were to service, the harder it was to justify the Charlestown yard's existence. The failure of the Navy to carry through modernization plans, including one whereby the majority of the yard's industrial activity would be transferred to an enhanced South Boston facility, helped to hasten the inevitable. Many associated with the yard also suspected that Massachusetts, as the only state going Democratic in the 1972 presidential election, would pay a penalty for failing to back the winner.

On April 16, 1973, the yard commander, Captain R. L. Arthur, announced that the Charlestown yard, along with the yard at Hunter's Point in San Francisco, was to close. Over the next year it ceased all fleet servicing and manufacturing operations, and on July 1, 1974, nearly 175 years of service to the nation ended with a formal disestablishment ceremony. Only one naval activity remained at Charlestown: the protection and maintenance of the old warship long associated with the yard, U.S.S. *Constitution*.

Top: *The launching of a ship celebrates the time, energy, and skill spent in its making. Here U.S.S.* **Guest,** *one of 24 destroyers built at Charlestown during World War II, slips into Boston Harbor in 1942. The big* **Fletcher**-*class destroyer took only five months to build.*

Bottom: *A destroyer is traditionally named for a distinguished naval figure, and if possible the closest female relative sponsors the namesake ship. In a centuries-old ritual, DD-461's sponsor Eileen Fairfax Thomson breaks a bottle of champagne against the ship's bow in 1941, sending it down the ways with the words, "I christen thee* **Forrest,** *and may God bless all who sail in her." Captain French Forrest commanded the Charlestown-built* **Cumberland** *in the Mexican War. Siding with the Confederates during the Civil War, he oversaw conversion of the burned U.S.S.* **Merrimack** *into the ironclad C.S.S.* **Virginia**—*destroyer of* **Cumberland** *(see pages 28-29).*

Ships for World War II

From 1933 to the end of World War II, the Charlestown yard moved outside its traditional role as repair yard and became a shipbuilding facility. It began with destroyers—ships it had long specialized in repairing—averaging two a year in the 1930s. This period of steady production was preamble to the World War II crash building program. Charlestown launched almost 200 vessels, including 24 destroyers, between 1939 and 1945. In 1942 it began building destroyer escorts—smaller, less expensive versions of

destroyers designed to counter German submarines. The final big program was the production of LSTs (Landing Ship, Tank) for amphibious assaults in Europe and Asia. LSDs (Landing Ship, Dock) for carrying other vessels; submarines; and various auxiliary vessels

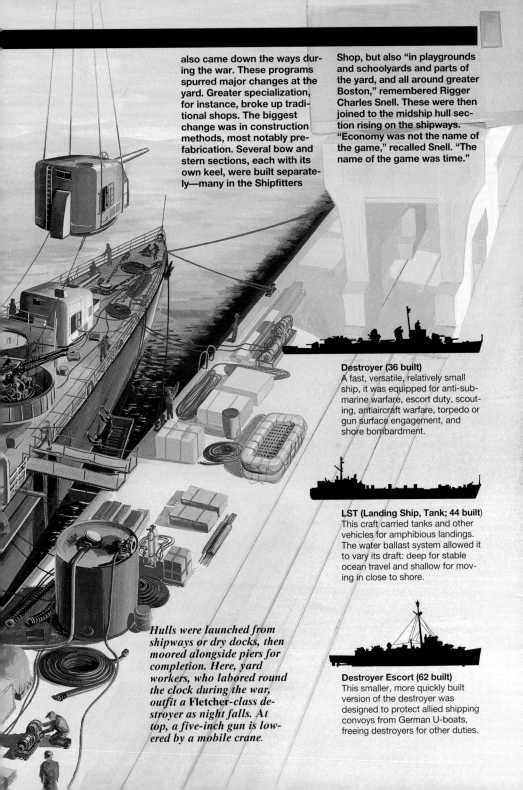

also came down the ways during the war. These programs spurred major changes at the yard. Greater specialization, for instance, broke up traditional shops. The biggest change was in construction methods, most notably prefabrication. Several bow and stern sections, each with its own keel, were built separately—many in the Shipfitters Shop, but also "in playgrounds and schoolyards and parts of the yard, and all around greater Boston," remembered Rigger Charles Snell. These were then joined to the midship hull section rising on the shipways. "Economy was not the name of the game," recalled Snell. "The name of the game was time."

Destroyer (36 built)
A fast, versatile, relatively small ship, it was equipped for anti-submarine warfare, escort duty, scouting, antiaircraft warfare, torpedo or gun surface engagement, and shore bombardment.

LST (Landing Ship, Tank; 44 built)
This craft carried tanks and other vehicles for amphibious landings. The water ballast system allowed it to vary its draft: deep for stable ocean travel and shallow for moving in close to shore.

Destroyer Escort (62 built)
This smaller, more quickly built version of the destroyer was designed to protect allied shipping convoys from German U-boats, freeing destroyers for other duties.

Hulls were launched from shipways or dry docks, then moored alongside piers for completion. Here, yard workers, who labored round the clock during the war, outfit a Fletcher-class destroyer as night falls. At top, a five-inch gun is lowered by a mobile crane.

During the long era of wooden sailing ships, when naval technology changed only gradually over the decades, a warship's service lasted as long as the materials from which it was built. But as the pace of change quickened in the mid-19th century with the advent of steam propulsion and iron hulls, a vessel quickly grew obsolete without continual incorporation of the latest technology. This state of affairs, which intensified in the 20th century, provided Charlestown Navy Yard with a new role after World War II: lengthening or transforming the careers of old ships, otherwise destined for mothballs, through modernization and conversion. Modernization meant updating old electrical, propulsion, or weapons systems or performing structural surgery without altering the vessel's function. This ranged from installing a sonar dome on the bottom of the hull *(below)* to dismantling the entire superstructure and building a new one. The process normally took several months. Conversion, which could take years, involved major alteration of a vessel to prepare it for a different tactical mission. A typical example

In the late 1950s the Navy began installing sonar equipment in bow domes. Bow domes reduced hull resistance and were less susceptible to bubble noise. The Charlestown yard, already a leader in sonar technology, *performed a prototype dome installation in 1958. To install a dome, workers first cut away part of the old bow (above), then fitted the prefabricated dome (right, on U.S.S. Willis A. Lee in 1961).*

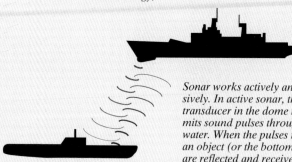

Sonar works actively and passively. In active sonar, the transducer in the dome transmits sound pulses through the water. When the pulses reach an object (or the bottom), they are reflected and received by the transducer as echoes. Distance is determined by time elapsed between transmission and echo. In passive sonar, hydrophones pick up noises generated by underwater sources.

would be the conversion of a conventional scouting, escorting, and submarine-fighting destroyer to a radar picket destroyer, whose role was to provide mid-ocean radar warning. A notable postwar task undertaken by the yard was the 1956 conversion of the destroyer *Gyatt* into the world's first guided missile destroyer. Basically, the vessel's aft five-inch guns were replaced with a twin missile launcher. But the ship had to be significantly altered to perform its new function. The yard designed automated systems that first affixed a booster charge to the missile and then moved it from the air-conditioned belowdecks magazine to the launcher. The decks and superstructure had to be reinforced to withstand the tremendous pressure and temperature of a launch. A system of ducts and blowout plates was installed to minimize damage and injury in the event of a premature explosion. Innovative retractable fins at midships helped stabilize the vessel for firing. With these and other changes, the yard remade *Gyatt* into a sophisticated missile-firing machine.

Part 2

Visiting Charlestown Navy Yard

The yard offers the visitor a captivating glimpse into the activities that for nearly two centuries supported the United States Navy. Here on the home front, thousands of civilian workers and navy personnel built, repaired, and supplied warships from the majestic sailing vessels of the early 19th century to the powerful steel navy of the 20th century. In 1974, the year of its closing, 30 acres of the historic yard were set aside for the National Park Service as a living museum of the Navy's activities here. The remaining 100 acres continue to be developed as part of the revitalization of Boston's waterfront.

Nineteenth-century buildings, docks, and piers reflect the yard's 174-year history. The commandant's 1805 hilltop mansion overlooked the activities below. Within view are Dry Dock 1, used by U.S.S. *Constitution* as early as 1833 and as late as 1995, the 1842 Carpenter Shop, the 1852 Pitch House (Building 10) for caulking wooden vessels, the 1833 Officers' Quarters, the 1813 Navy Stores (Building 5), and the 1811 Marine Barracks.

Two venerable warships, the 1797 frigate U.S.S. *Constitution* and the powerful 1943 destroyer, U.S.S. *Cassin Young*, float alongside the working piers, illustrating the changing United States Navy. Both the *Constitution*, an active duty Navy warship, and *Cassin Young*, maintained by National Park Service rangers and volunteers, offer free tours daily.

A National Park Service exhibit, "Serving the Fleet," and tours of the yard *(above right)* provide visitors with opportunities to explore the history of the site. The USS Constitution Museum offers a rich collection of artifacts, paintings, and models relating to the history of "Old Ironsides." The museum, located inside the Dry Dock 1 Pumphouse, is open daily to visitors.

Preceding pages: *U.S.S.* Cassin Young *at Pier 1.*

▮▮▮▮	Historic structure
Supply	Historic building name
G 149	Historic building letter or number
▮▮▮▮	Non-historic structure
	Freedom Trail (route subject to change)
	National Park Service boundary
	Public open space
P	Parking

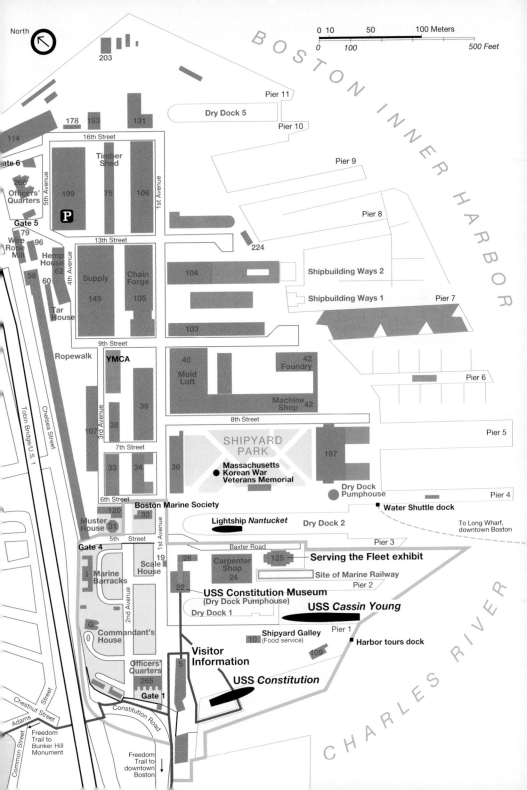

North

0 10   50   100 Meters
0   100   500 Feet

BOSTON INNER HARBOR

CHARLES RIVER

203

Pier 11
Dry Dock 5
Pier 10
Pier 9
Pier 8

178 193   131
114
16th Street
Gate 6
Timber Shed
266
Officers' Quarters
5th Avenue
199   75   106
1st Avenue
P
Gate 5
13th Street
79
Wire Rope Mill
96
Hemp House
62
58   60
4th Avenue
Supply
149
Chain Forge
105
Tar House
9th Street
Ropewalk
YMCA
3rd Avenue
107   38   39
7th Street
33   34
6th Street
120   32
Muster House
31
5th Street
Gate 4
Marine Barracks
2nd Avenue
1st Avenue
Boston Marine Society
19
28   Scale House
22   Carpenter Shop
24
125
Commandant's House
Officers' Quarters
265
Gate 1
Constitution Road

Pier 7
224
Shipbuilding Ways 2
104
Shipbuilding Ways 1
103
Pier 6
40   42 Foundry
Mold Loft
Machine Shop   42
8th Street
Pier 5
36
SHIPYARD PARK
Massachusetts Korean War Veterans Memorial
197
Dry Dock Pumphouse
Pier 4
Water Shuttle dock
To Long Wharf, downtown Boston
Lightship Nantucket
Dry Dock 2
Pier 3
Baxter Road
Serving the Fleet exhibit
Site of Marine Railway
Pier 2
USS Constitution Museum
(Dry Dock Pumphouse)
Dry Dock 1
USS Cassin Young
Pier 1
Shipyard Galley
10 (Food service)
Harbor tours dock
109
Visitor Information
USS Constitution

Tobin Bridge/U.S. 1
Chelsea Street
Chestnut Street
Adams Street
Common Street
Freedom Trail to Bunker Hill Monument
Freedom Trail to downtown Boston

Charlestown Navy Yard's buildings reflect the range of architectural styles employed over its long history. These structures served a variety of functions within the working yard, which was home to naval officers and their families as well as an industrial work place.

Beginning in 1853, the civilian shipyard workers living in surrounding communities, primarily Charlestown, assembled each morning to the ringing of the bell atop the octagonal Muster House *(top)*. For most of the 19th century, the workers mustered there three times daily, in the morning at sunrise, at lunch, and once more in the evening before retiring to their homes at sunset.

Directing the activities was the shipyard commandant, who lived with his family and personal staff in the impressive mansion *(middle)* constructed in 1805. Built on the yard's high ground, the Commandant's House provided a bird's-eye view of the construction and repair activities going on below. Today the house is open to the public for special tours, and numerous activities, such as historical military encampments *(bottom)*, take place on the expansive lawn through the summer months.

The Chain Forge *(above)* houses the massive hammers once used to forge die-lock chain, a unique process developed here in 1926. The country's only remaining full-length ropewalk *(left)* was for more than 130 years the sole facility in the Navy manufacturing rope for U.S. warships. Both buildings (not open to the public) await restoration and preservation work as part of the National Park Service's ongoing efforts to preserve the significant industrial heritage of the Charlestown Navy Yard.

The Navy's oldest commissioned warship, United States Ship *Constitution* and the Charlestown Navy Yard share a long history. Constructed in Boston between 1794 and 1797, "Old Ironsides" was repaired and supplied here many times during its active career. U.S.S. *Constitution* was permanently berthed in Charlestown in 1897 and has since been open to the public for tours. Like all wooden vessels, *Constitution* needs constant attention. In the 1920s, a major overhaul was capped with a nationwide tour. Between 1992 and 1995, *Constitution* underwent the most significant restoration to date in the yard's Dry Dock 1. Newly discovered drawings and descriptions were used to help skilled naval shipwrights restore the vessel to its original appearance. *Constitution* settles on dry dock blocks *(right)* in preparation for its 1990s restoration. Caulkers *(below right)* use traditional caulking hammers to seal the gun decks. *Below left* is a view off the bow of the venerable warship.

The World War II destroyer U.S.S. *Cassin Young* (DD-793) reflects a very different kind of sea power than does *Constitution*. Yet both warships, constructed 150 years apart, served much the same purpose. Like frigates, destroyers (known as the workhorses of the modern navy) are smaller and less powerful than the heaviest warships, but they are fast and remarkably versatile. Boasting five 5-inch guns and made of steel, *Cassin Young* was built on the West Coast in 1943 and took part in major Pacific engagements, including the Saipan landing and the Battle of Leyte Gulf, where its crew rescued over 100 sailors from the attack on U.S.S. *Princeton*. Aboard *Cassin Young*, "Rosie the Riveter" programs *(above)* introduce visitors to the work and lives of the women who wielded rivet guns and welding rods during World War II. Free tours *(above left)* let visitors see where the "tin can sailors" lived during their long months at sea. *Cassin Young*'s bow *(left)* offers views of the historic yard and harbor.

Today, exhibits and educational activities help bring alive the navy yard and Boston's maritime history. At the USS Constitution Museum *(top and middle)*, located in the historic Dry Dock 1 Pumphouse and adjacent buildings, hands-on activities help visitors to appreciate the skills of a 19th-century seaman and get a sense of his life aboard a sailing warship. Load and fire a replica cannon, try out a sailor's sleeping quarters, take a turn at the great wheel of a square-rigger, or command U.S.S. *Constitution* in battle on a computer screen.

The museum houses the frigate's logs, weapons, documents, charts, journals, decorative arts, and other items illustrating the epic role of "Old Ironsides" in U.S. history. Skilled craftsmen demonstrate ship model building, while films and special programs provide greater insight into the ship's story. A museum store offers other items relating to *Constitution's* history and to the nation's maritime heritage.

A permanent exhibit, "Serving the Fleet," which focuses on the history of the navy yard *(bottom)*, is open to the public on a seasonal basis in the navy yard's Paint Shop (Building 125).

National Park Service

The National Park Service is indebted to all those persons who made the production of this book possible. The text greatly benefited from suggestions by naval architect and historian John G. Arrison and historian Frederick R. Black. The primary source for the yard history was the National Park Service report, *The Charlestown Navy Yard 1800-1973* (*1800-1842* by Edwin C. Bearss; *1842-1890* by Edwin C. Bearss and Frederick R. Black; *1890-1973* by Frederick R. Black). Other important sources were Kenneth J. Hagan's *This People's Navy: The Making of American Sea Power*, 1991; Howard I. Chapelle's *The History of the American Sailing Navy*, 1949; and Donald L. Canney's *The Old Steam Navy*, 1990. The handbook was produced by the staff of the Division of Publications, National Park Service: Susan Barkus, designer; William Gordon, editor; Nancy Morbeck Haack, cartographer, assisted by the staff of Boston National Historical Park.